༄༅། །བཀའ་གདམས་པའི་དགེ་བ་ཤེས་
མཛོད་པའི་བློ་སྦྱོང་ཚིགས་བཅད་མ་བཞུགས་སོ།།

༡
བདག་ནི་སེམས་ཅན་ཐམས་ཅད་ལ།
ཡིད་བཞིན་ནོར་བུ་ལས་ལྷག་པའི།
དོན་མཆོག་སྒྲུབ་པའི་བསམ་པ་ཡིས།
རྟག་ཏུ་གཅེས་པར་འཛིན་པར་ཤོག།

༢
གང་དུ་སུ་དང་འགྲོགས་པའི་ཚེ།
བདག་ཉིད་ཀུན་ལས་དམན་བལྟ་ཞིང་།
གཞན་ལ་བསམ་པ་ཐག་པ་ཡིས།
མཆོག་ཏུ་གཅེས་པར་འཛིན་པར་ཤོག།

༣
སྤྱོད་ལམ་ཀུན་ཏུ་རང་རྒྱུད་ལ།
རྟོག་ཅིང་ཉོན་མོངས་སྐྱེས་མ་ཐག།
བདག་གཞན་མ་རུངས་བྱེད་པས་ན།
བཙན་ཐབས་གདོང་ནས་བཟློག་པར་ཤོག།

༤
རང་བཞིན་ངན་པའི་སེམས་ཅན་ནི།
སྡིག་སྡུག་དྲག་པོས་ནོན་མཐོང་ཚེ།
རིན་ཆེན་གཏེར་དང་འཕྲད་པ་བཞིན།
རྙེད་པར་དཀའ་བའི་གཅེས་འཛིན་ཤོག།

༥
བདག་ལ་གཞན་གྱིས་ཕྲག་དོག་གིས།
གཤེ་སྐུར་ལ་སོགས་མི་རིགས་པའི།
གྱོང་ཁ་རང་གིས་ལེན་པ་དང་།
རྒྱལ་ཁ་གཞན་ལ་འབུལ་བར་ཤོག།

༦
གང་ལ་བདག་གིས་ཕན་བཏགས་པའི།
རེ་བ་ཆེ་བ་གང་ཞིག་གིས།
ཤིན་ཏུ་མི་རིགས་གནོད་བྱེད་ནའང་།
བཤེས་གཉེན་དམ་པར་བལྟ་བར་ཤོག།

༧
མདོར་ན་དངོས་དང་བརྒྱུད་པ་ཡིས།
ཕན་བདེ་མ་རྣམས་ཀུན་ལ་འབུལ།
མ་ཡི་གནོད་དང་སྡུག་བསྔལ་ཀུན།
གསང་བས་བདག་ལ་ལེན་པར་ཤོག།

༨
དེ་དག་ཀུན་ཀྱང་ཆོས་བརྒྱད་ཀྱི།
རྟོག་པའི་དྲི་མས་མ་སྦགས་ཤིང་།
ཆོས་ཀུན་སྒྱུ་མར་ཤེས་པའི་བློས།
ཞེན་མེད་འཆིང་བ་ལས་གྲོལ་ཤོག།

TRANSFORMING THE MIND

TRANSFORMING THE MIND

Teachings on Generating Compassion

His Holiness the XIV Dalai Lama

Translated by Geshe Thupten Jinpa

Edited by Dominique Side and Geshe Thupten Jinpa

Thorsons

Thorsons
An Imprint of HarperCollins*Publishers*
77–85 Fulham Palace Road
Hammersmith, London W6 8JB

The Thorsons website address is: www.thorsons.com

Published by Thorsons 2000

3 5 7 9 10 8 6 4 2

A catalogue record for this book
is available from the British Library

ISBN 0 7225 4030 2 HB
ISBN 0 7225 3865 0 PB

Printed and bound in the United States of America by
R. R. Donnelley and Sons Company

Contents

PREFACE

IN MAY 1999 HIS HOLINESS THE DALAI LAMA
gave three days' teachings on *The Eight Verses on Transforming the
Mind* at the Wembley Conference Centre in London, and a public
talk entitled "Ethics for the New Millennium" at the Royal Albert
Hall. His Holiness' visit to the United Kingdom took place at the
request of the Tibet House Trust, UK.

At the invitation of the Archbishop of Canterbury, His Holi-
ness also delivered the 10th Lambeth Interfaith Lecture Towards a
Peaceful World, "The Role of Religious Communities," at Lambeth
Palace, London.

The Eight Verses on Transforming the Mind is one of the most
important texts from a genre of Tibetan spiritual writings known
as *lo-jong*, literally "transforming the mind." Written by the
eleventh-century Tibetan master Langri Thangpa, this short

work is referred to by His Holiness as one of his main sources of inspiration.

Central themes of the *lo-jong* teachings include, amongst others, the enhancement of compassion, the cultivation of balanced attitudes towards self and others, the development of positive ways of thinking, and the transformation of adverse situations into conditions favorable to spiritual development.

Four months before the actual events the tickets for both the teachings and the public lecture were sold out. Due to lack of space unfortunately many people were left disappointed. Subsequently, the Office of Tibet, London, has been approached by many to make the text of these teachings available to the wider public. We are, therefore, very happy to bring out this book today.

The Office of Tibet would like to thank Jane Rasch and Cait Collins for transcribing the teachings and Dominique Side for editing. We are grateful to Dr Thupten Jinpa for interpreting His Holiness' teachings into English and also for helping with the editing of the final manuscript.

MR MIGYUR DORJEE
REPRESENTATIVE OF HIS HOLINESS THE DALAI LAMA
IN LONDON

Chapter One

THE BASIS OF TRANSFORMATION

The Meaning of Transformation

THE TIBETAN TERM LO-JONG LITERALLY MEANS "training the mind" or "transforming the mind" and implies some kind of inner discipline. The whole point of transforming our heart and mind is to find happiness. When we speak about happiness and suffering, we are of course talking about our experience of happiness and suffering, so we are dealing with something that has a direct bearing on the human mind. Leaving aside the philosophical question of whether or not there is such a thing called consciousness that is distinct from our physical body, what is clear is that, as human beings, we all have the natural desire to be happy and the wish to overcome suffering. This is a fact, so we can make it our starting-point.

Before developing this point in more detail, however, let us look very briefly at the nature of experience. I think that we can definitely say that experience takes place at the level of consciousness or mind, because even though we talk about physical experiences, they do not stem from the body alone. If we numb a particular part of our body, for example, we can no longer feel, so experience is related to feeling, and feeling in turn is related to consciousness. Broadly speaking, our experiences fall into two categories. One type of experience is more connected with our bodies, and occurs mainly through our sense organs, while the other type is more related to what can be called "the mental consciousness" or "the mind."

So far as the physical level of experience is concerned, there is not much difference between ourselves and other animal species. Animals, too, have the capacity to feel both pain and well-being. But what perhaps distinguishes us human beings from other forms of life is that we have far more powerful mental experiences in the form of thoughts and emotions. Now of course, we could speculate that there are certain species of animal that may also be capable of having this kind of experience, at least to some degree—some animals may be capable of memory, for instance—but on the whole, it is fair to say that human beings have a greater capacity to experience things on the mental level.

The fact that there are two broad categories of experience has some interesting implications. Most importantly, if a person's basic state of mind is serene and calm, then it is possible for this inner peace to overwhelm a painful physical experience. On the

2

other hand, if someone is suffering from depression, anxiety, or any form of emotional distress, then even if he or she happens to be enjoying physical comforts, he will not really be able to experience the happiness that these could bring. So this shows that our state of mind, in terms of our attitudes and emotions, plays a crucial role in shaping the way we experience happiness and suffering. The *lo-jong* teachings on transforming the mind offer a series of methods by which we can channel and discipline our mind, and so create the basis for the happiness we are seeking.

We all know that there is an intimate connection between physical well-being and emotional well-being. We know, for example, that physical illnesses affect our state of mind, and that, conversely, a greater degree of physical well-being contributes towards greater mental ease. Since we commonly recognize this correlation, many of us engage in physical practices and exercises to help bring about that physical well-being which will contribute to our mental refreshment. There are also certain traditional practices that are aimed at training our energy patterns; these are called *prana yogas*, or "yogas of the wind energy." These days, yogic exercises have become very popular in the modern world, too, and this is precisely because many people have found that through yoga they can achieve a degree of physical health that leads to better mental health.

The approach that is suggested by the *lo-jong* teachings is slightly different, however. They concentrate directly on the development of the mind itself, through the transformation of our attitudes and ways of thinking.

It is important to realize that any practice which actually transforms our hearts and minds is not something that can be imposed or forced upon us. In the case of physical exercises, on the contrary, some degree of pressure may be very effective in establishing discipline, but the mental discipline required for the transformation of our hearts and minds cannot come about as a result of force. It has to be based on voluntary acceptance which, in turn, will be based on a personal recognition that certain attitudes and certain ways of being are beneficial, whereas others are not. Only then, on recognizing this, do we voluntarily take it upon ourselves to follow a spiritual discipline. This way of engaging with a spiritual path is the only way that will transform our minds.

It follows that the key to transforming our hearts and minds is to have an understanding of the way our thoughts and emotions work. We need to learn how to identify the opposing sides in our inner conflicts. With anger, for example, we need to see how destructive anger is, and, at the same time, realize that there are antidotes within our own thoughts and emotions that we can use to counter it. So, first, by understanding that afflictive thoughts and emotions are destructive and negative, and, second, by trying to strengthen our positive thoughts and emotions, which are their antidotes, we can gradually reduce the force of our anger, hatred and so on.

However, when we decide to work with our anger and hatred, it is not sufficient simply to make a pious wish: "May anger not arise in me" or "May I be free from hatred." Although this may be helpful, wishing alone won't really get you very far. You need to make a concerted effort to follow a conscious discipline, one that you apply throughout your life, to reduce the force of your anger and enhance its opposite, altruism. This is the way to discipline the mind.

The way to examine how thoughts and emotions arise in us is through introspection. It is quite natural for many different thoughts and emotions to arise. Why this should be is, of course, a philosophical question. According to Buddhist philosophy, many of them arise from past habits and *karma*, which give rise to an individual's propensity for thinking and feeling. However that may be, the fact is that various thoughts and emotions do arise in us, and when we leave them unexamined and untamed this leads to untold problems, crises, suffering and misery.

This is why we need to adopt the conscious discipline we spoke of earlier: in order to reduce the power of a negative emotion like anger or hatred, we need to encourage its antidote, which is love and compassion.

It is not enough to recognize that this is what is required, just as it is not enough simply to wish that love and compassion should increase in us. We have to make a sustained effort, again and again, to cultivate the positive aspects within us, and the key here is constant familiarity. The nature of human thoughts and emotions is such that the more you engage in them, and the more you develop them, the more powerful they become. Therefore we have to develop love and compassion consciously in order to enhance their strength. We are, in fact, talking about a way of cultivating habits that are positive. We do this through meditation.

Meditation: A Spiritual Discipline

What do we understand by meditation? From the Buddhist point of view, meditation is a spiritual discipline, and one that allows you to have some degree of control over your thoughts and emotions.

Why is it that we don't succeed in enjoying the lasting happiness that we are seeking? And why are we so often faced with suffering and misery instead? Buddhism explains that our normal state of mind is such that our thoughts and emotions are wild and unruly, and since we lack the mental discipline needed to tame them, we are powerless to control them. As a result, they control us. And thoughts and emotions, in their turn, tend to be controlled by our negative impulses rather than our positive ones. We need to reverse this cycle, so that our thoughts and emotions are freed from their subservience to negative impulses, and so we ourselves, as individuals, gain control of our own minds.

The idea of bringing about such a fundamental change in ourselves may at first sight seem impossible, yet it is actually possible to do this through a process of discipline such as meditation. We choose a particular object, and then we train our minds by developing our ability to remain focused on the object. Normally, if we just take a moment to reflect, we will see that our mind is not focused at all. We may be thinking about something and, all of a sudden, we find that we have been distracted because something else came into our head. Our thoughts are constantly chasing after this and that because we don't have the discipline of having a focus. So, through meditation, what we can achieve is the ability to place our minds and to focus our attention at will on any given object.

Now of course, we could choose to focus on a negative object in our meditation. If, for example, you are infatuated with someone, and if you focus your mind single-pointedly on that person, and then dwell on their desirable qualities, this will have the effect of increasing your sexual desire for that person. But this is not what meditation is for. From a Buddhist point of view, meditation has to be practiced in relation to a positive object, by which we mean an object that will enhance your ability to focus. Through that familiarity you become closer and closer to the object and feel a sense of intimacy with it. In the classical Buddhist literature this type of meditation is described as *shamatha*, tranquil abiding, which is a single-pointed meditation.

Shamatha alone is not sufficient. In Buddhism, we combine single-pointed meditation with the practice of analytic meditation, which is known as *vipasyana*, penetrative insight. In this practice we apply reasoning. By recognizing the strengths and weaknesses of different types of emotions and thoughts, together with their advantages and disadvantages, we are able to enhance our positive states of mind which contribute towards a sense of serenity, tranquillity, and contentment, and to reduce those attitudes and emotions that lead to suffering and dissatisfaction. Reasoning thus plays a helpful part in this process.

I should point out that the two types of meditative approach I have outlined, the single-pointed and the analytic, are not distinguished on the grounds that they each rely on a different type of object. The difference between them lies in the way each is applied, not in the objects chosen.

To clarify this point I will use the example of meditation on impermanence. If a meditator remains single-pointedly focused on the thought that everything changes from moment to moment, that is single-pointed meditation, whereas if someone meditates on impermanence by constantly applying, to everything he or she encounters, the various reasonings concerning the impermanent nature of things, reinforcing his conviction in the fact of impermanence through this analytic process, then he is practicing analytic meditation on impermanence. Both share a common object, impermanence, but the way in which each meditation is applied is different.

I feel that both types of meditation are actually practiced in almost all major religious traditions. In the case of ancient India, for instance, the practice of single-pointed meditation and the application of analytic meditation are common to all the major religious traditions, both Buddhist and non-Buddhist. During a conversation with a Christian friend of mine some years ago, I was told that in Christianity, and particularly in the Greek Orthodox tradition, there is a strong and long history of contemplative meditation. And similarly, a number of Jewish Rabbis have spoken to me about certain mystic practices in Judaism which involve a form of single-pointed meditation.

It is therefore possible to integrate both types of meditation into a theistic religion. A Christian, for instance, might engage in contemplation by reflecting upon the mysteries of the world, or the power of God's grace, or on various reasons that he or she finds deeply inspiring and that enhance his belief in the divine Creator. Through such a process the individual might arrive at a deep-felt faith in God, and then could rest his mind in that state and remain single-pointedly focused. In this way, the practitioner arrives at a single-pointed meditation on God through an analytic process, so both aspects of meditation are present.

Obstacles to Meditation

Buddhist texts speak of four principal obstacles that one must overcome for meditation to be successful. The first is mental scattering or distraction, which arises at the coarse level of mind and refers to the tendency for our thoughts to be scattered. The second obstacle is dullness and drowsiness, or the tendency to fall asleep. The third is mental laxity, which means that our mind is unable to retain sharpness and clarity. Finally, at a more subtle level, there is mental excitement, or agitation which stems from the fluctuating, changeable nature of our mind.

When our mind is too alert it becomes excitable and easily agitated, and then our thoughts go chasing after different ideas or objects which make us feel either elated or depressed. Too much excitement leads to all kinds of moods and emotional states. By contrast, when laxity arises it brings a sense of respite, so it can feel quite pleasant because it is restful. Despite this, however, it is actually an obstacle to meditation. I have noticed that when birds and animals are well fed they are completely relaxed and contented, so when we hear a well-fed happy cat purring away, we could say that it is in a state of mental laxity.

Mental dullness occurs at a coarser level of the mind, whereas mental laxity, which is in a sense a result of dullness, is experienced on a much more subtle level. In fact, it is said that it is difficult for a meditator to distinguish between genuine meditation and mental laxity. This is because in mental laxity there is still a degree of clarity. You have not lost the focus of your attention in the meditation, but there is no alertness. So although you have a kind of clarity in your perception of the object, there is no vitality in that state of mind. For a serious meditator, it is very important to be able to distinguish between subtle laxity and genuine meditation. This is all the more critical because there are said to be different degrees of mental laxity.

The other obstacle we spoke of is a scattered, distracted state of mind, and this refers to the very general problem we have as soon as we try to focus on a particular object. We find that our mind very quickly loses its power of attention, and gets distracted and carried away by ideas or memories that can be pleasant or unpleasant. The fourth obstacle, mental excitement, is a subcategory of distraction, but it refers more specifically to distractions associated with pleasant objects. The reason for specifying this as a separate class is because pleasant thoughts are what distract us most from meditation. They can be recollections of a past experience or of something that we have enjoyed, or thoughts about something we would like to experience. Memories and thoughts of this kind are often major factors which interfere with successful meditation.

Of these four obstacles, the two principal ones are distraction and mental laxity.

How do we deal with these obstacles? Dullness, in particular, seems to be closely connected with our physical state, so for example if we are deprived of sleep we can experience dullness. If we don't follow a suitable diet, be it in terms of what we eat or the quantities we eat, this can also bring about a state of dullness. It is for this reason that ordained members of the Buddhist monastic order are advised not to eat after lunch. By refraining from doing this monks and nuns can maintain a certain clarity of mind that is conducive to meditation, and they will also have a mental sharpness when they wake up the following morning. So good dietary behavior is a very effective antidote for mental dullness.

If we turn now to the problem of mental laxity, it is said that the reason laxity arises in meditation is because we are not alert enough, and because our energy is low. Whenever this happens we need to find a way of lifting our spirits, and one of the best ways of doing this is to cultivate a sense of joyfulness by reflecting on our achievements, or on the positive aspects of life, and so forth. This is the chief antidote for laxity.

Generally speaking, mental laxity is said to be a neutral state of mind, in the sense that it is neither virtuous nor non-virtuous (that is, it gives rise to neither virtuous nor non-virtuous thoughts and actions). However, at the start of the meditation session the mind might begin in a virtuous state. For example, a meditator can be focusing single-pointedly on the impermanent nature of life, and then, at a certain point, he begins to lose the alertness of that focused mind and lapses into mental laxity. At the beginning of his practice, however, his state was virtuous.

Agitation arises when our state of mind is too uplifted and we are over-excited. The antidote for this is to find a way of bringing that excited state down to a more sober level. One way is to reflect on thoughts and ideas which have a naturally sobering effect, like death and the transient nature of life, or the fundamentally unsatisfactory side of human existence.

These methods can be applied, of course, in the context of almost all the major religious traditions. For example in the case of a theistic religion, if one finds there is too much dullness and mental laxity in one's meditation, then one can uplift one's state of mind by contemplating on God's grace, or on the great compassionate nature of the Divine Being. These thoughts can instill in you a sense of joy, and lift your mind out of its dullness. Similarly, if there is too much excitement in your meditation, then reflecting on how you are often unable to live according to God's precepts and teachings, or remembering original sin, can immediately bring a sense of humility that will temper your elation. In this way, the practices can be adapted and incorporated into different religions.

To summarize, we have seen that in order to counter the four obstacles to meditation, and particularly the two principal ones, distraction and mental laxity, what is required is the skillful application of two important mental faculties: mindfulness and introspection. Through introspection we develop a vigilance that enables us to see whether, at any given moment, our mind is under the influence of excitement or distraction, and whether it is focused or lapsing into dullness. Once we have observed our state of mind, mindfulness allows us to bring our attention back to the object of meditation and to remain focused on it. So we could say that the practice of mindfulness is the essence of meditation.

Whatever forms of meditation you practice, the most important point is to apply mindfulness continuously, and make a sustained effort. It is unrealistic to expect results from meditation within a short period of time. What is required is continuous sustained effort.

Regardless of whether the actual term is used or not, analytic meditation is in fact applied in everyday life, in almost every profession. Take the example of a businessman. To be successful, he has to have sharp critical faculties, examine all the pros and cons in negotiations, and so forth, so whether he is conscious of it or not, he is applying the very same analytical skills that we use in meditation.

Generally, of the two types of meditation, I would say that it is analytic meditation that seems to have a greater effect in bringing about the transformation of heart and mind.

The Nature and Continuum of Consciousness

On the first line of the Tibetan text of *The Eight Verses on Trans-forming the Mind* (see English text in Appendix I), the first word is "I" (*dag*). It is very important to ask ourselves what exactly we understand by this term. To do this, we have to situate the teachings of the Buddha within the broad context of the various spiritual traditions of India. One point that sets the Buddhist teaching apart from all other classical Indian traditions is that it rejects any notion of an eternal soul or self, or *atman*, defined as something independent of our physical and mental reality, unitary, unchanging and permanent.

Buddhists argue that what we call the self or the person can only be understood as a function of our psycho-physical constituents.[1] These are the "aggregates" which together make up our existence. If we examine the nature of these mind–body aggregates, we find that they are constantly changing, therefore the self cannot be unchanging; they are also transient, so the self cannot be permanent or eternal; and they are diverse and multiple, so the self cannot be unitary. It is on these grounds that Buddhism rejects the notion of an eternal unchanging soul.

Since all Buddhist schools maintain that the existence of the self has to be understood as a function of the individual's physical and mental constituents, this means that the self should not be

---

[1] There are five *skandhas*, or psycho-physical constituents, in Buddhist psychology, namely form (the body), feeling, perception, mental formations, and consciousness. The first relates to the body, and the other four relate to the mind.

considered purely at the gross level of the body. In fact Buddhist schools usually define the self in relation to the continuum of consciousness.

There is another question that commonly arises with regards to the self. Does the self have a beginning and an end, or not?

Some Buddhist schools, such as the Vaibhashika school, seem to accept the notion that it is possible for the continuum of self to come to an end. However, most traditions maintain that it has neither beginning nor end, on the grounds that the self is understood in relation to the continuum of consciousness, and Buddhist schools generally assert that we cannot posit a beginning to consciousness. If we were to posit a beginning to consciousness, then we would have to accept a first instant of consciousness that is uncaused and has come from nowhere. This would contradict one of the fundamental principles of Buddhism, which is the law of cause and effect. Buddhism accepts the dependent nature of reality, according to which everything arises as a result of the coming together of certain causes and conditions, so if consciousness could come into being from no cause, this would go against that fundamental principle. Buddhists therefore consider that every instance of consciousness must be produced by causes and conditions of some kind. Of the many causes and conditions in question, the main or substantial cause of consciousness must be some form of experience, since matter alone cannot produce consciousness. Consciousness must come from a previous instance of consciousness.

Likewise, if we try to trace the origin of the material world, we find that, at least from the Buddhist point of view, the world is also without beginning. Through analysis, we can reduce a physical object to its constituent elements, then to its molecules, its atomic parts, and so on, but even these must be produced by causes and conditions of their own.

Just as the mind is said to be without beginning, so it is also said to be without end, because there is nothing that can undermine the basic existence of our faculty for knowing and experiencing. Certain states of mind, such as sensory experiences, are contingent upon our physical body, and these may come to an end when their physical basis ceases to exist, say, at the point of death. However, when we speak of the continuum of consciousness being without beginning, we should not confine our understanding of consciousness to the gross level of existence. Rather, what Buddhists are referring to is a subtler level of consciousness, especially what we call "the luminous nature of mind," and it is this that we say is continuous and has no end. So it is on this basis that Buddhists argue that the self has no beginning and no end.

Generally, when people think about consciousness they tend to have the impression that there is some kind of monolithic entity called "mind." However, that is not the case. If we probe a little deeper, we will see that what we call "consciousness" actually covers a diverse and complex world of thoughts, emotions, sensory experiences, and so forth.

Let me illustrate this point by looking at the way we perceive things. In order for perception to occur at all, certain conditions must be present. In the case of a visual perception, for example, an external object must come into contact with the physical organ, our eyes, to produce a perceptual event. Then there must be a further condition that allows the sensory organ to interact with the object in such a way that the event gives rise to a cognition. Now Buddhists would argue that the mind has an underlying luminous nature which is the "mere fact" of experience and awareness, and it is this continuum that allows cognitions to arise from the contact between the sense organs and their corresponding objects. Furthermore, it is this underlying luminous nature of mind that transcends the temporal existence of a particular lifetime, since it maintains an uninterrupted continuum. So this is what Buddhists understand by such terms as "the beginningless nature of consciousness" or "the continuum of consciousness."

As I mentioned earlier, Buddhists even talk about the physical world as being in some sense without beginning. "But what about the Big Bang?" you may ask. "Isn't that the beginning of the universe?" For a Buddhist it cannot be accepted as the real beginning of the physical world, and rather than being the solution to our problem it only raises more questions. For instance, why did the Big Bang occur at all? What are the conditions that led to the Big Bang? From a Buddhist point of view, even the physical world cannot be said to have an absolute beginning.

I should point out that when we say that the world has no beginning, we are referring to a very subtle "atomic" level. Furthermore, it is true, of course, that a particular universe or a particular planet will have a beginning in the sense that it comes into being at a particular point in time, and at another point it will cease to exist. When we say the physical world has no beginning, we are therefore talking of the universe as a whole.

So all this points us back to the fundamental principle of cause and effect. In order to fully appreciate this principle one must accept its relevance both on the minute level of individual events and on the wider macroscopic level. The reason that the Buddhist teachings emphasize the importance of cause and effect is not because it is some kind of divine law, but rather because it provides a deeper understanding of the nature of reality. Why do Buddhists come to this conclusion? Because we know from our experience, and through observation, that things and events do not arise randomly. They respect a certain order. There is a certain correlation between particular events and particular causes and conditions. Furthermore, things do not come about without any cause at all. Once we exclude these two possibilities of random existence and causelessness, we are forced to accept the third alternative, namely that there must be an underlying principle of causation operating at a fundamental level.

You might wonder why this understanding of cause and effect is so important for a Buddhist practitioner. The reason is because Buddhism places a tremendous emphasis on transforming the mind and heart, and on bringing about inner changes in our ways of being and understanding. Furthermore, in Buddhism, the methods of contemplation, meditation and transformation of the mind must be based on something that exists in reality. If reality is not in accord with our meditative practices, there is no real basis for expecting any progress in personal development. It is therefore by cultivating an understanding of the nature of reality, and through enhancing and developing that understanding, that we can begin to apply the meditation methods to ourselves and bring about an inner transformation.

In Buddhism, certain practices are followed to counter specific problems. For example, there are meditations that are designed to reduce the intensity of one's sexual desire and attachment. We might visualize the entire face of the Earth being filled with skeletons, for example. Such meditations are practiced deliberately to overcome specific types of problem, but in these cases the meditator does not believe in any way that the visualization represents reality. He or she is fully aware that this particular image is deliberately cultivated as a means of dealing with certain emotions.

In general, Buddhism highlights the importance of developing a reasoned understanding in relation to any chosen topic of enquiry. This is done on the simple premise that increasing our understanding of things will have a positive effect on our heart and mind, and that it is by enhancing our understanding and knowledge that change really takes place. Many profound levels of spiritual realization are therefore said to be the results of knowledge, insight, and understanding. This is why the development of insight is considered such a crucial element of the spiritual path as a whole.

THE FOUR SEALS OF BUDDHISM

I mentioned earlier that it is a basic fact of life that we all naturally and instinctively desire to be happy and overcome suffering. The wish to be happy is fundamental to all of us. As to why this is so, perhaps we can simply say, "That's the way it is." Although we all have this natural aspiration, however, and although what we long for is happiness, it is also a natural fact that over and over again we undergo painful experiences and face sufferings of various kinds. So why is this? Why, despite our deep desire to be happy, are we constantly confronted with suffering and pain instead?

From the Buddhist point of view, the reason is that we have certain fundamentally flawed ways of perceiving and relating to ourselves and to the world. At the root of this lie what Buddhism identifies as four false views. The first is to view things and events which are in reality impermanent and transient, as eternal, permanent and unchanging. The second is to view things and events which are actually sources of dissatisfaction and suffering as pleasurable and as true sources of happiness. The third false view is that we often tend to apprehend as pure and desirable things which are in reality impure. And the fourth false view is our tendency to project a notion of real existence upon events and things which in reality lack any such autonomy.

Fundamentally flawed views of reality lead to certain false ways of relating to the world and to oneself, which in turn lead to confusion, misery and suffering. On the basis of this dynamic, Buddhism formulates what are known as the Four Seals, a set of axioms which are common to all schools of Buddhism. The Four Seals are:

1 All composite phenomena are impermanent.
2 All contaminated phenomena are unsatisfactory.
3 All phenomena are devoid of self-existence.
4 Nirvana is true peace.

1 All composite phenomena are impermanent

One of the fundamental insights of Buddhism is the understanding that all things are impermanent; this is the first of the Four Seals. The point here is that all things that arise from causes and conditions are impermanent, and are in a process of continual flux.

As far as the gross level of impermanence is concerned, we are all aware of how certain things come to an end, how things go through a process of change, and so on. But the Buddhist would take this further, and argue that underlying the perceptible changes that we can all observe, there must be a subtler level of change, a process that may not be so evident. If we are to account for the observable changes that happen over a longer period of time, we should, in principle, be able to trace the process down to the smallest conceivable unit of time. Logically, then, even within a minute point of time there is a constant and dynamic process. Everything is going through this subtle process of change, even from one moment to the next. Therefore we can reason that anything that arises as a result of causes and conditions is, by nature, impermanent. In other words, anything that is conditioned must be transient.

Once you understand this fundamental point then you can begin to see that the happiness that we all aspire to achieve, and the suffering that we all instinctively want to avoid, are themselves experiences that result from causes and conditions. Happiness and suffering do not come from nowhere, they arise as a result of their own causes and conditions. This very fact suggests that although, for example, you may now be going through a painful experience, or even intense suffering, the very fact that your experience is conditioned means that it will pass. In this way we come to realize that both happiness and suffering are subject to change and are impermanent. In terms of their transient nature, then, there is a parity between happiness and suffering.

2 All contaminated phenomena are unsatisfactory

The second seal points out the difference between happiness and suffering, and states that all contaminated phenomena are fundamentally unsatisfactory. The implication is that those things that do not arise from such contaminated causes can be satisfying and fulfilling. When we talk about contaminated phenomena in this context, we are referring to events and experiences that arise under the power of negative impulses, or afflictive thoughts and emotions; they are called "contaminated" because they are tainted by the pollutants of the mind. This is why they are fundamentally unsatisfying, and why their nature is said to be *duhkha*, or suffering.

This second axiom does not simply refer to those physical sensations that we can all readily label as pain and suffering. Of course, the wish to be free of suffering is common to all of us, but there are different ways of understanding what suffering is, depending on one's level of awareness. When Buddhists speak about overcoming suffering, especially in the context of the second seal, we are referring to a very subtle level of suffering. Those who are familiar with the way Buddhism classifies the various types of suffering will know that three levels are identified: the suffering of suffering, the suffering of change, and the suffering of pervasive conditioning. It is this third level of suffering that we are dealing with in the second seal.

As I mentioned, one of the implications of this second axiom is that if we are free of mental pollutants, then we can gain the lasting, genuine happiness that we long for. The question is, why is the nature of the pollutants such that they render a particular experience one of suffering? And is it possible to overcome these pollutants, these negative thoughts and emotions?

Mental pollutants, or afflictive thoughts and emotions, refer to a whole class of thoughts and emotions that are afflictive by nature. The etymology of the Tibetan word *nyon-mong* suggests something that afflicts us from within, "afflicting" meaning that it causes suffering and pain. The point here is that at the root of all our sufferings, at the subtlest level, lie the afflictions of mind— negative impulses, negative thoughts and emotions, and so forth. This suggests that the root of suffering lies within us, and the root of happiness also lies within us. The key insight we draw from this is that the degree to which we are able to discipline our mind is what determines whether we are happy or whether we suffer. A disciplined state of mind, a spiritually transformed state of mind, leads to happiness, whereas an undisciplined state of mind that is under the power of the afflictions, leads to suffering.

We can now combine together our contemplations on these first two seals. From the first seal, that all composite phenomena are impermanent, we gained the insight that anything that comes into being as a result of causes and conditions is not only dependent on other factors for its existence, but also exists within a process of continual change with no real power to stand on its own. Furthermore, the process of change does not itself require any other third factor to put it into motion; rather, the causes and conditions that give rise to the origination of a thing are the very causes and conditions that also plant the seed for its cessation. To summarize, whatever is conditioned lacks any independent power of its own; it is therefore called "other-powered," and is determined by forces other than itself. Now, if we combine that insight with the second seal, we realize that anything that arises as a result of contaminated causes and conditions—the mental pollutants— is fundamentally unsatisfactory, and is under the power of these pollutants.

By reflecting in this way, we come to recognize the fact that we allow ourselves to be ruled and controlled by our thoughts and emotions and, furthermore, that we allow our thoughts and emotions to be determined by our negative impulses and other afflictions of the mind. We therefore begin to realize that if we continue to allow this situation to occur, it can only lead to misery and suffering. By thinking along these lines, we will come to see our afflictive emotions and thoughts as truly destructive forces.

Whatever brings disaster or harm should be called an enemy, so this means that the ultimate enemy is actually within ourselves. This makes things so difficult! If our enemy is out there, outside, we can try to run away or hide. We might even be able to deceive him sometimes. But if the enemy is within ourselves, it is so difficult to know what to do. So the critical question for a spiritual practitioner is whether or not it is possible for this inner enemy to be overcome. This is also our main challenge.

If it is the case, as suggested by some ancient philosophers, that the pollutants lie in the very nature of consciousness itself, and are inseparable from it, then so long as consciousness exists these pollutants will exist as an essential characteristic of our mind. This implies that there is no possibility of overcoming them. If this were true, I would personally rather be a hedonist. I wouldn't make any effort to follow a spiritual path but would seek solace in alcohol, or maybe some other substances, and forget about the whole idea of spiritual training. Also, I would not bother to engage in these probing philosophical questions. Maybe, after all, that is the best way to be happy. If you compare human beings with animals, for example, sometimes we humans are so caught up in our imagination and thinking that we create our own complications, while animals who do not indulge in these intellectual activities can seem quite content, calm, and relaxed. They eat, and when they are well fed, they sleep, and then they relax. From one point of view they seem to be much more content than we are. This question brings us to the third seal.

3 All phenomena are devoid of self-existence

The third axiom, that all phenomena are empty and are devoid of self-existence, should not be understood in a nihilistic way. You should not think that the Buddhist teachings state that, in the final analysis, nothing exists. This cannot be the case, because in fact we are talking about suffering, about happiness, and about the best means to fulfill our aspiration to be happy and overcome suffering, so we are certainly not suggesting that nothing exists. What the third seal does indicate is rather that there is a fundamental disparity between our perception of the world and ourselves, and the way things actually are. Things do not exist in the manner in which we tend to believe that they do, as an independent, objective reality out there.

In order to address the question of whether or not negative emotions such as anger, hatred, and so forth, really reside in the essential nature of our minds, we examine ourselves and our experience. Is anger present in every instant of our conscious state? Is hatred there continually, all the time? We find that they are not. Sometimes anger arises, sometimes hatred arises, and then they disappear. It is not the case that whenever consciousness is present these negative emotions are present as well. Anger and hatred do arise, but sometimes their opposites, love and compassion, arise instead. Buddhism infers from this that the basic consciousness is clouded by whatever thoughts and emotions occur at a given moment. We also make the point that two mutually conflicting emotions, like love on the one hand and hatred on the other, cannot co-exist in a single instant in the same person. This implies that various thoughts and emotions occur in our minds at different moments, which means that our negative emotions do not reside in us as ever-present, inseparable parts of our basic mind. This is why we say that thoughts and emotions arise and then cloud the basic mind. We therefore consider that the basic mind is neutral; it can be influenced by positive thoughts and emotions, or, on the other hand, by negative ones. So there are grounds for hope.

Now, on the basis of all this reasoning, the big question we must now turn to is whether afflictive emotions can actually be eliminated or not.

We saw earlier that change and transformation are possible by virtue of impermanence, which means that there is indeed a possibility of overcoming negative emotions and thoughts. However, the broader and more fundamental question is whether or not it is possible to eliminate these pollutants of mind completely. All schools of Buddhism argue that this is possible, and in fact, in many Buddhist teachings, we find a very extensive discussion of the nature of these afflictions, their destructive potential, their causes and conditions, and so on. The essence of these discussions should be understood in relation to the attempt to eliminate negative impulses altogether.

We can, of course, talk about Dharma in the context of ethics, and speak about refraining from killing, from lying, and so forth, and about engaging in virtuous activities. However, this is Dharma only in a very general sense of the word, since ethical guidelines are not particularly unique to the Buddhist teaching. The understanding of spiritual practice that is unique to Buddhism lies in this possibility of the total cessation of negative impulses. This is called nirvana—total relief from, and cessation of, the afflictions of mind. We could say that nirvana is the essence of Buddha-Dharma.

For a Buddhist practitioner, all aspects of Dharma practice have to be understood in the light of this ultimate spiritual aim of gaining freedom from the pollutants of mind. This also applies to ethics, ethical practices being steps towards the goal of liberation. Since the ultimate aim of a Buddhist is to eradicate all the negative emotions and thoughts that give rise to negative actions, the effort a practitioner makes to lead an ethical way of life indicates his or her commitment to dealing with negative thoughts and emotions. The first stage of this effort is to address the manifestations of these afflictions, namely physical and verbal behavior.

When we analyze the nature of our afflictive emotions and thoughts, we see that underlying all of these experiences are certain projections of our mind, certain imaginings, which occur irrespective of whether they have an objective basis or not. For example, in an object we consider desirable we will perceive certain desirable qualities and we may then exaggerate them through the power of our imagination. We then tend to dwell on them and indulge in them, all of which leads to developing a stronger and stronger attachment to that object of desire. Similarly, when we are confronted by objects that are undesirable, we again tend to project certain characteristics and properties onto them which are above and beyond objective reality, and as a result we will feel repulsed and want to draw away from them. These are the basic drives in operation when we interact with things; either we feel attracted or we feel repulsed. These drives lead to all the other types of emotional response that we have to events and objects. So there is a dynamic in process, underlying which is a strong clinging to objects, whether the clinging be expressed through desire or through repulsion. This gives rise to all our afflictions.

Within the various Buddhist schools there are different understandings of the nature of these afflictions and what causes them, depending on their respective views of the nature of reality. It seems that the philosophically more advanced schools of Buddhism have a more profound understanding of our afflictions. For example, the great Indian master Nagarjuna said that nirvana must be understood as freedom from mental afflictions and from the karmic actions to which they give rise. Suffering is caused by our karmic actions, and these in turn are motivated by the underlying forces of negative thoughts and emotions. These, in their turn, are produced by our projections and imaginings, which are themselves rooted in a false perception of reality. The false perception of reality here refers to perceiving things and events as enjoying some kind of objective, real, independent existence.

According to Nagarjuna, insight into emptiness is what really dispels this fundamental ignorance or misperception of the world, so this point relates directly to the third axiom: that all phenomena are empty and devoid of inherent existence. This axiom tells us that although our normal perception leads us to believe that things are permanent and real, and enjoy some kind of independent existence, through analysis we find that in reality they lack these qualities. We therefore discover that any perception suggesting that things exist inherently and independently is a false perception, and that only insight into emptiness can cut through this misperception and dispel it. Many of the negative thoughts and emotions which take root in our flawed way of viewing reality will therefore be eliminated when this insight is generated, and when we see through our perceptions and recognize them to be false.

We can now summarize all these points in the following way. By means of personal reflection, we come to realize that the basic mind, or the nature of consciousness, is neutral; it is neither negative nor positive. We also find that many of our negative thoughts and emotions have their root in our fundamentally flawed way of understanding the reality of the world and of ourselves. Then we find that insight into emptiness counters such misperception. Furthermore, we realize that negative emotions on the one hand, and insight on the other, directly oppose each other: the difference between them is that the latter is grounded in, and supported by, valid experience and reasoning, while the former does not have a valid grounding in either reason or experience. So, by bringing all of these points together, we develop a sense that by cultivating insight into emptiness it is possible to eliminate all our mental afflictions.

4 Nirvana is true peace

The fourth seal points to the fact that the essential nature of mind is pure and luminous. False perceptions, and negative thoughts and emotions, do not reside in the essential nature of mind. Given that the afflictions are rooted in false perception, there is an antidote that can eliminate them: this is insight into the emptiness of all things, or true perception of reality. Therefore emptiness, which is the absence of inherent existence, is sometimes referred to as "natural nirvana." It is because the nature of phenomena is empty that true nirvana, true freedom from suffering, is possible.

This explains why the Buddhist scriptures present four types of nirvana: natural nirvana, which refers to emptiness; a nirvana "with residue," which generally refers to the continued physical existence of the individual; nirvana without residue; and finally, non-abiding nirvana. It is on the basis of natural nirvana that all the other levels of nirvana are possible.

The precise meaning of nirvana with residue and without residue is explained differently by the various schools of Buddhism. Some speak of the residue as the physical aggregates of the individual, while others refer to the residue of dualistic perceptions. The residue of the physical aggregates refers to the physical constituents that the individual has acquired as a result of previous karma. However, I will not go into a detailed discussion of these here.

So, basically, from the third seal we realize that the fundamental nature of reality is that it is devoid of inherent existence. All phenomena that result from other factors lack inherent independent existence, yet we view them falsely as being autonomous. This misperception lies at the root of much of our confusion and also gives rise to afflictive thoughts and emotions. Insight into the nature of reality reveals things as devoid of inherent existence, and acts as a direct antidote to false perception, and consequently to the afflictions of the mind. The total elimination of all negative thoughts and emotions, and their underlying false perceptions, is what is meant by nirvana.

The Tibetan term for nirvana is *nyang-de*, which literally translates as "beyond sorrow." In this context sorrow refers to the afflictions of the mind, so nirvana really refers to a state of being that is free from afflictive thoughts and emotions. Nirvana is freedom from suffering and from the causes of suffering. When we perceive nirvana in these terms, we begin to realize what true and genuine happiness really means. We can therefore envisage the possibility of being totally free from suffering.

So we can conclude by reiterating that insight into emptiness is what enables us to dispel and eliminate our negative thoughts and emotions, as well as the false perceptions that underpin them. It is in emptiness that all of these pollutants are cleansed and purified. The main point, then, is that a Buddhist understanding of nirvana must be based on an understanding of emptiness.

The Question of Validating the Path

When you consider the reasoning I have just outlined, you might think it all sounds fairly rational and seems to make good enough sense. But what evidence do we have to show that these arguments are valid and that their logic is meaningful? Is there a proof that we can observe or experience?

On this question, I would like to refer to an explanation that I find personally helpful, which is taught in the Sakya teachings,[2] in the *Lam dre* tradition of Path and Fruition. According to this, there are four valid factors of knowledge, namely valid scripture, valid treatises or commentaries, valid teacher, and valid experience.

In terms of their origin, of course, the valid scriptures were taught first, and the valid commentaries were elaborated on them later. Then, on the strength of their study, valid teachers emerged who became masters of those commentaries. This led to their having valid experiences. However, from the point of view of the development of one's own personal conviction it is suggested that this order is reversed—in other words, one must first begin with some kind of personal experience. If we take the case of reflecting upon the Four Seals, or the empty nature of phenomena, or the benefits of altruism, unless we have some taste or personal experience of the theme, that is, unless we have a glimpse of its truth, it is less likely that we will be inspired deeply enough to persist in our practice.

[2] The Sakya school is one of the four main schools of Tibetan Buddhism.

Of course, there are many different levels and degrees of spiritual experience. There are profound levels of realization, which I for one may not have, but there is also a beginning level which we all have. In my own case, whenever I contemplate on the virtues of compassion and altruism I feel deeply moved. But how can we know that such experiences are valid? One way is to look at the effects they have upon us. When we reflect on certain spiritual qualities and cultivate them, and when we begin to feel deeply inspired, this creates a sense of inner strength. This experience makes us more courageous, more expansive, and less prone to worry or insecurity. All these are indications of the validity of our experience.

So, as I mentioned before, reflecting on certain spiritual qualities often moves me deeply, and this profound inspiration then increases my admiration of the masters who personify these values. Contemplating in this way, I begin to recognize that perhaps there is some truth in the biographies of the great masters and in their accounts of profound spiritual realization. No doubt we have to accept that anecdotal accounts and biographies are often prone to exaggeration, especially in the case of over-enthusiastic presentations of a guru's qualities by his own disciples. However, we cannot dismiss an entire category of literature on the grounds that it is untrustworthy. This cannot be the case—there must be some accounts of masters that relate to genuine experiences.

Indeed, this is not the only instance of exaggeration in the Buddhist literature. When I read a very sophisticated commentary written by a great scholar on a short text written by one of his

masters, the commentary is sometimes so detailed and comprehensive that I begin to wonder whether the author of the original
short text really had all these points in mind!

So when you can relate to the experiences narrated in the
biographies of the masters from the vantage point of your own
personal experience, you begin to develop deep admiration for
the valid masters. From valid experience, then, you proceed to
valid masters, and once you respect the valid masters, you then
develop conviction in the treatises they have written, which in
turn helps you to develop a deep conviction in the basic source of
the teachings, namely the Buddhist scriptures. I personally find
this way of approaching the teachings very helpful: you start from
your personal experience, which constitutes the cornerstone of
your spiritual practice.

For a Buddhist practitioner, especially for a Mahayana practitioner, it is vital to have deep admiration for the Buddha, and
that admiration must be grounded in a profound understanding
of the essence of his teaching, the Dharma. The understanding of
Dharma should itself be based on the understanding of selflessness or emptiness that I mentioned earlier. To perceive the Buddha merely as a historical person who was a great teacher, with
admirable and extraordinary qualities and immense compassion,
is not the perspective of a serious practitioner. A Buddhist's
appreciation of the Buddha should be grounded in knowledge of
his central and most profound teaching, which is emptiness.
Such a person should realize that buddhahood, or complete
enlightenment, is the embodiment of the four *kayas* or four

"Buddha-bodies."[3] This principle should itself be understood in relation to another fundamental point which is that, at the deepest level, mind and body are non-dual. Therefore the fully enlightened state should be understood as the total non-duality of wisdom and compassion.

To sum up the discussion so far, the Four Seals or axioms of the Buddhist teachings tell us that the suffering that none of us wishes to experience comes about as a result of afflictive thoughts and emotions, which in turn have their roots in false views. The four main false views are holding things to be permanent, believing impermanent things will bring happiness, holding things to be desirable, and believing that things enjoy independent existence. These views can all be eliminated, and this is done by developing insight into the true nature of reality. As you cultivate this insight and enhance it, false views are gradually eradicated along with their derivative thoughts and emotions. This process requires discipline. It is through such a process that transformation takes place.

In terms of the actual method of bringing about a transformation of heart and mind, the Buddhist tradition explains that there are two main dimensions to the path, which are known as "the method aspect" and "the wisdom aspect." One could say that the method aspect, which includes the various skillful means

[3] The Sanskrit word *kaya* means "body" in the sense of a body or embodiment of numerous qualities. The four *kayas* are: Svabhavikakaya, the Buddha-body of enlightened nature; Jnanakaya, the Buddha-body of perfect wisdom; Sambhogakaya, the Buddha-body of perfect resource; and Nirmanakaya, the Buddha-body of perfect emanation.

employed on the path, is a preparatory phase. It enables the practitioner subsequently to apply the wisdom or insight that eliminates negative afflictions directly.

QUESTIONS

Question: In a busy city lifestyle, it's sometimes tempting to remove oneself to go and meditate somewhere peaceful and leave the world behind. Would you say it is more important to stay with one's normal lifestyle or to give in to the temptation to escape it?

HHDL: It depends very much on the individual. If the person is a very advanced practitioner who is totally committed to a single-minded life of meditation and retreat, then of course there could be cases where the individual should seek a life of solitude and abandon the world, as it were. That is said to be the highest form of spiritual practice. But this is not appropriate for all practitioners. In fact, practitioners of this calibre are very rare.

Generally, for practitioners like ourselves, it is far more important to be an effective member of society, someone who makes a positive social contribution and integrates spiritual practice as much as possible into daily life. One must simply find time in the morning or in the evening to do some contemplative practices, meditation and so forth. For most of us that's the best way. Otherwise what can happen is that people escape from society and spend some time alone, and later begin to realize that actually it's a very hard thing to do. Then slowly and quietly, and with some embarrassment, they try to sneak back into society!

Question: What type of meditation would Your Holiness suggest for beginners?

HHDL: Reflect on impermanence, and if you have some wider knowledge then reflect on the nature of suffering. You could also contemplate the nature of cessation. Actually, contemplating on the Four Noble Truths is the foundation of the Buddha Dharma, so begin by reflecting along these lines rather than visualizing yourself as a deity! Mantras only keep our lips busy; for a beginner, I think there is a certain limitation to mantra practice. A master from Amdo, in eastern Tibet, once said that when you recite mantras too much, while plying your rosary beads, instead of diminishing your negative emotions it might only serve to diminish your nails!

Question: Your Holiness, please speak about prayer from a Buddhist perspective. If there is no deity, to whom or what do you pray?

HHDL: Usually we appeal to higher beings, like buddhas, bodhisattvas, and others, who are more powerful than us. That's the Buddhist way. But these higher beings were not higher beings from the outset; originally, they were like ourselves, and then through the training of their own minds they eventually became buddhas and bodhisattvas. That is how we understand it.

Question: Can we combine the Tibetan repetition of mantras and various visualizations with the practice of *vipasyana*—not in the same session, mixing the two, but in different parts of the day? I feel I need the two practices. Is this wrong? Can you give us your ideas on how to do this?

HHDL: Of course it is perfectly possible to combine the two practices. Even from the point of view of the Tibetan Buddhist path, the core practice is really the contemplations carried out within *vipasyana* practice. The Vajrayana practices of reciting mantras and doing visualizations are complementary to this; they enhance the actual practice which is the contemplation.

    There is a danger that people get the impression that in order to practice Buddhism in the Tibetan way you need all the ritual aspects of it, such as blowing the long horns, or playing the clarinet and cymbals, and so on, but this really isn't the essence of the practice. In fact I used to tell people, including Tibetans, that perhaps one of the greatest exemplary figures in Tibetan history, whose life embodies the true practice of Tibetan Buddhism, was the great meditator Milarepa. Yet if someone had searched his meditation cave I'm sure they wouldn't have found any long horns, cymbals or clarinets.

It is said that when the Indian master Atisha came to Tibet in the eleventh century, he was met by a large congregation of Tibetan lamas. There was a huge reception, and he saw them approaching from a distance. They were very impressive-looking lamas, on horses that were very ornately decorated with all sorts of colourful garments and bells, and the lamas themselves were wearing impressive costumes with colourful hats. Some hats were even shaped like a bird's head. Atisha was so surprised and shocked that he cried, "Ah! The Tibetan ghosts are coming," and hid his face. He didn't want to look; he thought it was an hallucination. The Tibetans got the message, so they descended from their horses, sent the horses away, and changed into simple monastic robes. When they then approached the Indian master, he was pleased to meet them.

Many Tibetans know this story, and we recount it constantly, over and over again. Yet somehow, despite this, we seem to get caught up in colorful ritual

THE BASIS OF TRANSFORMATION

paraphernalia. When I was in Lhasa, of course, I
would dress in expensive silk brocades. But I think
if we pay too much attention to these things, both
the teachings and the rituals themselves become
superficial and come to lose their meaning.

Since we became refugees we have had a very good
opportunity to change these things. I have stopped
wearing all these expensive clothes. The simple
monk's robe I wear is very good, easy to wash and
very comfortable! Brocade is very rough on the skin
and is not easily washable, and especially in the
Indian heat it gets dirty very easily! So circumstance
itself has made it impossible to wear such elaborate
clothes, and I think that's very fortunate! I am sure
that if one were to inspect one of those vests the
monks wear in Tibet, one could almost guarantee
that the dirt collected on the collar would go back
several generations! I think such things are really
foolish. We repeat the Buddha's name, but by
carrying out these practices we neglect the Buddha's
instruction, and that is very sad.

Whether we follow a religion or not is entirely a
matter of individual choice; but if we want to follow
one, then we should take it seriously, and practice it
wholeheartedly. That is important. So I feel the time
has now come for Buddhists to re-examine some of
their traditional habits. The same goes for other

religious traditions, too. Once you accept a religion, you should be serious and sincere, and put it into practice in your day-to-day life. Then it will be of some value. If religious faith is just a custom it is not much use.

Chapter Two

TRANSFORMING THROUGH ALTRUISM

The Qualities of Bodhichitta, the Altruistic Intention

THE EIGHT VERSES ON TRANSFORMING THE MIND
by Geshe Langri Thangpa (see Appendix I) is a teaching on the
practice of *bodhichitta*, the altruistic intention to attain full
enlightenment for the benefit of all sentient beings. Before we go
into these verses in detail, let us try and understand what we mean
by bodhichitta.

The definition of *bodhichitta* is given in Maitreya's *Ornament of
Realization (Abhisamayalamkara)*, where he states that there are
two aspects to altruism. The first is the condition that produces
the altruistic outlook, and this involves the compassion that a person must develop towards all sentient beings, and the aspiration
he or she must cultivate to bring about the welfare of all sentient

beings. This leads to the second aspect, which is the wish to attain enlightenment. It is for the sake of benefitting all beings that this wish should arise in us.

We could say that *bodhichitta* is the highest level of altruism and the highest form of courage, and we could also say that *bodhichitta* is the outcome of the highest altruistic activity. As Lama Tsongkhapa explains in his *Great Exposition of the Path to Enlightenment* (*Lam rim chen mo*), *bodhichitta* is such that while one engages in fulfilling the wishes of others, the fulfillment of one's own self-interest comes as a by-product. This is a wise way of benefitting both oneself and others. In fact I think *bodhichitta* is really and truly wonderful. The more I think of helping others, and the stronger my feeling for taking care of others becomes, the more benefit I reap myself. That is quite extraordinary.

Elaborating further on the positive qualities of *bodhichitta*, we find that it is one of the most effective means of accumulating merit and enhancing our spiritual potential. Furthermore, it is one of the most powerful methods for countering negative tendencies and destructive impulses. Since overcoming negative tendencies and enhancing positive potential are the very essence of the spiritual path, the practice of developing altruism is really the greatest, most effective and most compelling practice of all.

Maitreya also states in one of his aspirational prayers that it is this same *bodhichitta* that can free us from transmigration into the lower realms of existence, that can lead us to higher and more fortunate rebirths, and that can even lead us to the state beyond aging and death. Maitreya is implying something very special here. Generally, according to the Buddhist teachings, it is the practice of morality and ethical conduct which protects us from rebirth in the lower realms of existence. What Maitreya is saying is that the practice of *bodhichitta* surpasses all ethical practices and is, in fact, a far superior path. Similarly, he states that *bodhichitta* is a superior path when it comes to planting the seeds for attaining higher forms of rebirth.

So in a sense we could say that the practice of generating and cultivating the altruistic intention is so comprehensive that it contains the essential elements of all other spiritual practices. Taken alone, it can therefore replace the practice of many different techniques, since all other methods are distilled into one approach. This is why we consider that *bodhichitta* practice lies at the root of both temporary and lasting happiness.

If you look at the precepts that are taken by a practitioner of *bodhichitta* you will see the tremendous courage that underlies this practice. In his *Precious Garland* (*Ratnavali*), Nagarjuna writes:

May I always be an object of enjoyment
For all sentient beings according to their wish
And without interference as are the earth,
Water, fire, wind, medicine and forests.

May I be as dear to sentient beings as their
Own life and may they be very dear to me,

May their sins fructify for me
And all my virtues for them.[1]

It is clear that a tremendous amount of courage is reflected in these sentiments. The courage of such expansive altruistic thinking reaches out to all beings without exception, and is not confined to any particular time. It is completely unlimited. In a verse of his *Guide to the Bodhisattva's Way of Life* (*Bodhicaryavatara*) Shantideva also expresses this tremendous courage, which transcends all boundaries of space and time. He writes:

As long as space endures,
As long as sentient beings remain,
Until then, may I too remain
And dispel the miseries of the world.

When the altruistic intention is supported by insight into emptiness, and particularly by the direct realization of emptiness, one is said to have attained the two dimensions of *bodhichitta* which are known as conventional and ultimate *bodhichitta*. With both these practices of compassion and wisdom, the practitioner has within his or her hands the complete method for attaining the highest spiritual goal. Such a person is truly great and worthy of admiration.

[1] *The Precious Garland and The Song of the Four Mindfulnesses*, Nagarjuna and the 7th Dalai Lama, (translated by Jeffrey Hopkins), Wisdom of Tibet Series 2, George Allen & Unwin, London, 1975. Stanzas 483 and 484, page 90.

If one is able to cultivate these spiritual qualities within oneself then, as Chandrakirti writes very poetically in his *Entry to the Middle Way* (*Madhyamakavatara*), with one wing of altruistic intention and another wing of insight into emptiness, one can traverse the whole of space and soar beyond the state of existence to the shores of fully enlightened buddhahood.

Although I have some experience of these two dimensions of *bodhichitta*, I feel that I have very little realization of them. Nevertheless, I have a real desire and enthusiasm to practice, and that itself inspires me immensely. As I have mentioned on many occasions, I believe that we are all fundamentally the same, and have the same basic potential. Some of you, I have no doubt, have a much better brain than mine. You should therefore make an effort to contemplate, study and meditate, but without any short-sighted expectations. You should have the same attitude as Shanti-deva—that as long as space exists you will remain to dispel suffering in the world. When you have that kind of determination and courage to develop your capacity, then a hundred years, an aeon, a million years are nothing to you. Furthermore, you will not consider that the different human problems we have here and there are in any way insurmountable. Such an attitude and vision bring some kind of real inner strength. You might think that it is a delusion to think in this way, but even if it is, that doesn't matter—I find it helpful!

Now the question is how we can train ourselves to develop *bodhichitta*. The two aspects of *bodhichitta* that we spoke about earlier, the aspiration to be of help to others and the aspiration to attain enlightenment oneself, have to be cultivated separately through separate trainings. The aspiration to be of help to others has to be cultivated first.

The wish to bring about the welfare of others can, of course, include relieving them from their very obvious sufferings and physical pain, but this is not what is meant in this context. Bringing about others' welfare really means helping them attain liberation. We must therefore begin with an understanding of what is meant by liberation. This relates back directly to what I described earlier, namely the understanding of emptiness, because nirvana as defined by the Buddhist teachings has to be understood in terms of emptiness. So, according to Buddhism, without some understanding of emptiness it is not really possible to understand what true liberation is; and without that, a strong aspiration to attain liberation will not arise.

The second aspiration, to attain full enlightenment, is also directly related with one's understanding of emptiness. The Tibetan word for enlightenment is *chang-chub*, and the Sanskrit is *bodhi*. Looking at the etymology of the two Tibetan syllables, *chang* means "purification" or "purified," and this refers to a quality of the fully enlightened Buddha, indicating that all negative characteristics and mental pollutants have been overcome. The second syllable, *chub*, literally means "having realized," and this refers to the Buddha's quality of having perfected all knowledge and realization. So, enlightenment, as expressed in the Tibetan term *chang-chub*, suggests both overcoming our negative qualities and perfecting our positive ones. This is directly connected to one's understanding of emptiness, for it implies that one realizes that it is possible to eliminate the negative aspects of the mind, and it assumes some degree of understanding of how this can be done and of what the nature of total freedom is.

The Way of the Intelligent Practitioner

I explained earlier that the scriptures which outline the actual practice for training the mind present two main aspects of the path, the method aspect and the wisdom aspect. Generally, as far as the presentation and understanding of the method aspect are concerned, there are no substantial differences between the various Buddhist schools, although there can be differences in emphasis with respect to particular practices. But as far as the wisdom aspect is concerned, there are real differences between the schools and between the various scriptural texts.

Many scriptures are attributed to the historical Buddha, yet later Buddhist schools, particularly the Mind Only (Cittamatra) school and the Middle Way (Madhyamaka) school, distinguished two different categories of texts, even within the corpus of scriptures which contains the Word of the Buddha. These schools state that there are scriptures that can be taken at their literal face value, and those which cannot be accepted as literal but which require further interpretation. On what grounds can we determine whether a scripture is of literal or non-literal meaning? If we were to rely on another scripture to make this distinction, this would simply raise a further question: on what grounds could we take the adjudicating scripture itself at face value? This would lead to an infinite regress. What this suggests is that, in the final analysis, one can only rely on one's own understanding, experience, and reasoning. Therefore, in Buddhism, critical thinking is a crucial element in one's understanding of the scriptures. It is to make this important point that the Buddha himself is quoted as saying:

> *Just as people test the purity of gold by burning it in fire, by cutting it and examining it on a touchstone, so exactly you should, O ye monks, accept my words after subjecting them to a critical test and not out of reverence for me.*

This suggests that there are two main ways of approaching the Buddhist teachings, according to the capacity of the practitioner: the intelligent way and the less intelligent way. The intelligent way is to approach the scriptures and their commentaries with skepticism and an open mind, and to subject the content of these teachings to investigation by relating them to one's own personal experience and understanding. Then, as one's understanding grows, one's conviction in the content of the scriptures will also grow, along with one's admiration for the Buddha's teaching in general. Such a person will not follow a teaching or a scripture just because it is attributed to a famous master or someone worthy of respect; rather, the contents of the scripture will be judged valid on the basis of that person's own understanding, derived through personal investigation and analysis.

The Buddhist principle of the Four Reliances applies to this intelligent approach. These are expressed as follows:

> *Rely on the message of the teacher, not on the person of the teacher;*
> *Rely on the meaning, not just on the words;*
> *Rely on the definitive meaning, not on the provisional one;*
> *Rely on your wisdom mind, not on your ordinary mind.*

In other words, you should not rely on a master's fame, status and so on, but rather on what is said; you should not rely on the words themselves, but on their meaning; you should not rely on the provisional meaning, but on the definitive meaning; and finally, you should not rely on mere intellectual understanding of the meaning, but rather on a deep experience and realization. This is the intelligent way of approaching the Buddhist teachings.

Therefore, as you approach the next part of this teaching, I suggest that you try to retain the attitude of open skepticism that I have just spoken about.

The Two Altruistic Aspirations

1 The aspiration to attain enlightenment

As we have seen, the highest form of spiritual practice is the cultivation of the altruistic intention to attain enlightenment for the benefit of all sentient beings, known as *bodhichitta*. This is the most precious state of mind, the supreme source of benefit and goodness, that which fulfills both our immediate and ultimate aspirations, and the basis of altruistic activity. However, *bodhichitta* can only be realized through regular concerted effort, so in order to attain it we need to cultivate the discipline necessary for training and transforming our mind.

As we discussed earlier, the transformation of mind and heart does not happen overnight but through a gradual process. Although it is true that in some cases instantaneous spiritual experiences may be possible, they are rather unreliable and somewhat shortlived. The problem is that when sudden experiences occur, like bolts of lightning, the individual may feel profoundly moved and inspired, but if the experiences are not grounded in discipline and sustained effort they are very unpredictable, and their transformative impact will be rather limited. By contrast, a genuine transformation that results from sustained concerted effort is long-lasting because it has a firm foundation. This is why long-term spiritual transformation can really only come about through a gradual process of training and discipline.

We have seen that the altruistic intention is endowed with the dual aspiration to help other sentient beings and to attain enlightenment for their sake. First we discussed the need to have a basic understanding of what is meant by enlightenment. I explained how the Tibetan word for enlightenment, *chang-chub*, is composed of two syllables, one relating to the abandoning of negativities and the other to the perfection of positive qualities. We can now further our understanding of enlightenment by considering the presentation made by Maitreya in his *Sublime Continuum* (*Ratnagotravibhaga*). He states that all the pollutants of our mind are adventitious, meaning that they can be separated from the essential nature of mind. This indicates the possibility of being able to eliminate the afflictions of mind and heart, that is, afflictive emotions and thoughts. Maitreya then makes the point that as far as the enlightened qualities of the Buddha are concerned, we all possess within us the potential or seed for their perfection. This means that the potential for perfection, the potential for full enlightenment, actually lies within each one of us. In fact this potential is nothing other than the essential nature of the mind itself, which is said to be the mere nature of luminosity and knowing. Through the gradual process of spiritual practice, we can eliminate the obstructions that hinder us from perfecting this seed of enlightenment. As we overcome them, step by step, so the inherent quality of our consciousness begins to become more and more manifest until it reaches the highest stage of perfection, which is none other than the enlightened mind of the Buddha.

According to Buddhism, there are two types of adventitious pollutants. The first are the manifest afflictions of mind, which take the form of our negative thoughts and emotions, while the second type is known as the subtle obstructions to knowledge. These are the imprints and propensities produced by the repeated occurrence of negative thoughts and emotions in us. Since we have already seen that it is possible to eradicate negative thoughts and emotions, this implies, by extension, that we will also be able to overcome the propensities created by their repeated occurrence. Once we appreciate this point, we will have a sense of what is meant by enlightenment in the Buddhist sense. I pointed out in Chapter 1 that a proper understanding of the nature of complete enlightenment depends on a good understanding of emptiness.

The teachings of many of the other ancient spiritual traditions of India also contain a notion of nirvana, *moksa*, or spiritual freedom. It also seems that some traditions identify these states with a physical realm of existence. However, as far as the Buddhist understanding of nirvana is concerned, it is a state of mind and not an external reality.

This is not to say that there is no divergence of opinion amongst the various Buddhist schools on the precise meaning of liberation. For example, the Vaibhashika school maintains that the historical Buddha Shakyamuni was fully enlightened and had overcome two of the four negative forces, namely afflictive emotions and thoughts, and the powerful forces of desire and attachment. However, it considers that Buddha had not overcome the other two negative forces—the force of death, and the force of the aggregates[2] of existence. The Vaibhashikas therefore understand final nirvana in terms of the total cessation of the individual. The implication is that when final nirvana is attained the individual being ceases to exist.

---

[2]   The five *skandhas* (see Chapter 1, note 1).

This view is not accepted by many other Buddhist schools. There is a very well-known objection by Nagarjuna, for example, who asserts that the logical consequence of the Vaibhashika view is that no one ever attains nirvana, because when nirvana is attained the individual ceases to exist. So this position is absurd. As we saw earlier, the person is simply a name given to the continuum of psycho-physical aggregates (the mind–body complex), and if this complex ceases to exist completely, then the person will cease to exist too. However, this view is not accepted by other Buddhist schools.

Similarly, there are many other aspects of the Vaibhashika doctrine that are rejected by other Buddhist schools. In their theory of knowledge, for instance, they reject the notion of sense data. They believe that sensory perceptions occur as a result of the mere interaction between the sense organs and the physical object, and that there are no sense data which act as a medium between the two. One of the objections raised against this theory is that it implies that for any vivid perception of an object to occur, the object in question must be physically present, and yet this is not always the case. From personal experience we know that sometimes we can have a very vivid recollection of an object, as if it were really there in front of us, and yet such a perception is due to the power of memory.

Again, the Vaibhashika understanding of the nature of consciousness at the point of death is a much coarser view than that of other schools. Adherents of this school believe that the state of mind at death can be virtuous, non-virtuous, or neutral. But other Buddhist schools have argued that the state of mind at the actual precise moment of death is always neutral, because it is a very subtle state. These are just a few examples of how uncritical the ideas of the Vaibhashika school can be compared to the much more refined understanding of other Buddhist schools.

Other schools argue that when one begins to purify the negative aspects of mind and body through the spiritual practice, and as one overcomes negative thoughts and emotions with their resulting propensities, and finally eliminates them altogether, one will also be perfecting one's psycho-physical aggregates. They therefore accept that as the pollutants of mind cease to exist, their manifestations and imprints—the impure body and mind—may cease to exist too. But this does not mean that the very continuum of the individual comes to an end. There is a subtle level of existence which is free of many of these manifest pollutants.

My point here is that there is a lot of debate on the exact nature of enlightenment. Basically, from the Buddhist point of view, the nature of true liberation and spiritual freedom has to be understood as a quality of mind, a freedom from the negative aspects and pollutants of mind.

According to Chandrakirti, a famous Indian teacher of the Middle Way school, liberation or true cessation is the ultimate truth. His point is that true cessation can only come about on the basis of understanding the ultimate nature of reality, that is, emptiness. So here we have a more refined understanding of nirvana, as arising from a sound understanding of emptiness. In this view, it is insight into the ultimate nature of reality that enables us to eliminate the pollutants of the mind. Furthermore, it is our ignorance of this ultimate nature of reality that lies at the root of all our obscurations, confusions and delusions. Finally, it is the emptiness of the mind in its perfected state that is true liberation. So the basis of true liberation is emptiness, the knowledge by which we eliminate our obscurations is that of emptiness, and the final perfected stage in which we attain liberation is the emptiness of mind.

When we say that it is the ultimate nature of mind that is liberation, we are not talking about the ultimate nature of mind generally, but specifically about the stage when the individual has overcome all the pollutants and the negative aspects of the mind. So true cessation has two dimensions: one is total freedom from mental pollutants, and the other is the total negation of inherent existence. We can illustrate this with the first verse of Nagarjuna's *Fundamental Wisdom of the Middle Way*[3] (*Mula-madhyamakakarika*):

I prostrate to the Perfect Buddha,
The best of teachers, who taught that
Whatever is dependently arisen is
Unceasing, unborn,
Unannihilated, not permanent,
Not coming, not going,

[3]   The Fundamental Wisdom of the Middle Way, translated by Jay L. Garfield, Oxford University Press, 1995, p. 2.

Without distinction, without identity,
And free from conceptual construction.

Nagarjuna pays homage to the Buddha by saying that Buddha taught the principle of dependent origination and emptiness. He describes cessation in terms of the total pacification of all conceptual elaborations; it is when all conceptual constructions have been pacified that there is true cessation.

2 Working for the welfare of others

The other aspiration of the altruistic intention (*bodhichitta*) is the wish to bring about the welfare of other sentient beings. Welfare, in the Buddhist sense, means helping others to attain total freedom from suffering, and the term "other sentient beings" refers to the infinite number of beings in the universe. This aspiration is really the key to the first, namely the intention to attain enlightenment for the benefit of all sentient beings. It is founded on genuine compassion towards all sentient beings equally. Compassion here means the wish that all other beings should be free of suffering. So it is said to be at the root of all altruistic activity and of the altruistic intention as a whole.

We need to cultivate a compassion that is powerful enough to make us feel committed to bringing about the well-being of others, so that we are actually willing to shoulder the responsibility for making this happen. In Buddhism, such compassion is called "great compassion." This point is emphasized again and again in the Mahayana literature, the fact that great compassion is the foundation of all positive qualities, the root of the entire Mahayana path, and the heart of *bodhichitta*. For example, Maitreya declares in his *Ornament of Sutras* (*Mahayanasutralamkara*) that compassion is the root of *bodhichitta*. Likewise, Chandrakirti says in his *Entry to the Middle Way* (*Madhyamakavatara*) that compassion is such a supreme spiritual quality that it maintains its relevance at all times: it is vital at the initial stage of the spiritual path, it is just as important while we are on the path, and it is equally relevant when an individual has become fully enlightened.

The point I am trying to make is that if we look at any Mahayana texts, we will find that compassion is not only highly praised, but the authors also repeatedly emphasize its importance in the sense that it really lies at the root of all spiritual endeavor. To cite a further example, in the opening verse of salutation to his *Compendium of Valid Cognition* (*Pramanasamuccaya*) Dignaga argues that the Buddha can be considered a valid spiritual teacher because he is the embodiment of compassion, and because he has perfected its development. So in fact, Dignaga uses the perfection of compassion as the basis for arguing that the Buddha is a valid spiritual teacher. Of course, having great compassion alone is not enough to be a true and authentic teacher, so Dignaga goes on to say that the Buddha also has direct realization of emptiness and has completely overcome all obstructions.

Generally speaking, as I said, compassion is the wish that others should be free of suffering, but if we look into it more closely compassion has two levels. In one case it may exist simply at the level of a wish—just wishing the other to be free of suffering—but it can also exist on a higher level, where the emotion goes beyond a mere wish to include the added dimension of actually wanting to do something about the suffering of others. In this case, a sense of responsibility and personal commitment enters into the thought and emotion of altruism.

Whichever level of compassion we may have, for the development of *bodhichitta* to be successful it must be combined with the complementary factor of wisdom and insight. If you lack wisdom and insight, when you are confronted with another's suffering, genuine compassion may arise in you spontaneously, but given that your resources are limited, you may only be able to make a wish: "May he or she be free of that pain or suffering." However, over time that kind of feeling may lead to a feeling of helplessness because you realize you cannot really do anything to change the situation. On the other hand, if you are equipped with wisdom and insight then you have a much greater resource to draw on, and the more you focus on the object of compassion, the greater the intensity of your compassion will be and the more it will increase.

Because of the way insight and wisdom affect the development of compassion, the Buddhist literature identifies three different types of compassion. First, at the initial stage, compassion is simply the wish to see other sentient beings freed from suffering; it is not reinforced by any particular insight into the nature of suffering or the nature of a sentient being. Then, at the second stage, compassion is not simply the wish to see another being free from suffering, it is strengthened by insight into the transient nature of existence, such as the realization that the being who is the object of your compassion does not exist permanently. When insight complements your compassion it gives it greater power. Finally, at the third stage, compassion is described as "non-objectifying compassion." It can be directed towards that same suffering being, but now it is reinforced by a full awareness of the ultimate nature of that being. This is a very powerful type of compassion, because it enables you to engage with the other person without objectifying him or her, and without clinging on to the idea that he or she has any absolute reality.

Since compassion is the wish that others should be free of suffering, it requires above all the ability to feel connected to other beings. We know from experience that the closer we feel towards a particular person or animal, the greater our capacity to empathize with that being. It follows, then, that an important element in the spiritual practice of developing compassion is the ability to feel empathetic and connected, and to have a sense of closeness with others. Buddhism describes this as a sense of intimacy with the object of compassion; it is also called loving-kindness. The closer you feel towards another being, the more powerfully you will feel that the sight of his or her suffering is unbearable.

There are two main methods in Buddhism for cultivating this sense of closeness or intimacy. One is the method known as "exchanging and equalizing oneself with others." Although it stems from Nagarjuna, it was more fully developed by Shantideva in his *Guide to the Bodhisattva's Way of Life* (*Bodhicaryavatara*). The other technique is known as the "seven-point cause and effect method." This emphasizes the cultivation of an attitude that enables us to relate to all other beings as we would to someone very dear. The traditional example given is that we should consider all sentient beings as our mother, but some scriptures also include considering beings as our father, or as dear friends, or as close relatives, and so on. Our mother is simply taken as an example, but the point is that we should learn to view all other sentient beings as very dear and close to our hearts.

It seems that for some the seven-point cause and effect method is more effective, while for others the technique of exchanging and equalizing self with others appears to be more effective, depending upon the individual's inclinations and mentality. However, within the Tibetan tradition the custom really has been to combine both these methods so that one can enjoy the benefits of practicing both approaches. For example, although the principal approach in *The Eight Verses on Transforming the Mind* is that of exchanging and equalizing self with others, the text refers to all sentient beings as "our mothers," suggesting that it also incorporates the seven-point cause and effect method.

The Seven-Point Cause and Effect Method

Before we can apply the seven-point cause and effect method[4] to ourselves, we need to cultivate a sense of equanimity towards all sentient beings, which is expressed through the ability to relate to all others equally. To do this, we need to address the problem of having thoughts and emotions that fluctuate. Not only should we try to overcome extreme negative emotions like anger and hatred, but also, in this particular spiritual practice, we should try to work with the attachment we feel to our loved ones.

Now, of course, in this attachment to loved ones there is a sense of closeness and intimacy, as well as an element of love, compassion and affection, but often these emotions are also tinged with a strong feeling of desire. The reason for that is rather obvious, because when we relate to people towards whom we feel deeply attached, our feelings are highly susceptible to emotional extremes. When such a person does something that is contrary to our expectations, for instance, it has a much greater potential to hurt us than if the same thing were done by someone to whom we do not feel that close. This indicates that in the affection we feel there is a high degree of attachment. So, in this particular spiritual practice, we try to level out the attachment we have to certain people, so that our sense of closeness to them is genuine and not tinged with desire.

---

[4] The seven points of this method are: recognizing that all sentient beings have been our mother in a past life; reflecting on the kindness of all beings; meditating on repaying their kindness; meditating on love; meditating on compassion; generating the extraordinary attitude of universal responsibility; and the actual development of *bodhichitta*.

The key point in this preliminary practice of equanimity is to overcome the feelings of partiality and discrimination that we normally feel towards others, based on the fluctuating emotions and thoughts associated with closeness and distance. It really seems to be true that attachment constrains our vision, so that we are not able to see things from a wider perspective.

Recently I was at a seminar on science and religion in Argentina, and one of the participant scientists made a point which I think is very true. His name is Mathurena, and he is the mentor of the neurobiologist Francisco Varela, whom I have known for a long time. He said that it is very important for research scientists to adopt the methodological principle of not being emotionally attached to their field of inquiry. This is because attachment has the negative effect of clouding and narrowing your vision. I totally agree. This is why, through the practice of equanimity, we try to overcome these feelings of partiality so that we can deal with everything and relate to everyone evenhandedly.

In this respect I would like to add how much I appreciate the general Western emphasis on objectivity, at least in the intellectual field. However, I do also detect a major contradiction here, because when I talk to people of various professional backgrounds, particularly from the West, they seem to have a tremendous amount of attachment to their own profession. One could say that many people seem to have an enormous personal investment in their profession, they identify with it, so much so that they feel as if their profession is so vital for the world's well-being that if it were to degenerate the whole world would suffer. This suggests to me that their level of attachment is inappropriate. Tsongkhapa, the great Tibetan master, once said that some people have a tendency to pick up one grain of rice and then, on the strength of an observation they make on it, conclude that all grains in the whole universe are just the same. Likewise, some professionals appear to have that kind of extreme attachment to their own narrow perspective. So there seems to be a contradiction between these two aspects of the Western mentality.

When we practice developing equanimity, sometimes it is helpful to use visualization. For example, you can imagine three different individuals in front of you: someone who is very close to you, someone you regard as an enemy and whom you dislike, and then someone who is completely neutral and to whom you feel indifferent. Then let your natural emotions and thoughts arise in relation to these three individuals. Once you are able to allow your natural feelings to arise, you will notice that towards the loved one you feel a sense of closeness and also great attachment, towards the person you dislike you may feel hostility and a sense of distance, and that towards the individual who is neutral you will hardly feel any emotion at all.

At this point, try to reason with yourself. "Why do I feel such different emotions towards these three individuals? Why do I feel so attached to my loved ones?" You might begin to see that there are certain grounds for your attachment: the person is dear to you because he or she has done this and that for you, and so on. But if you then ask yourself whether these characteristics are permanent and whether the person will always be like this, then you may have to concede that this is not necessarily the case. Someone may be a friend today but turn into an enemy tomorrow. This is especially true from the Buddhist point of view, when we take many lifetimes into account—someone who is very close to you in this life may have been your enemy in another. From this perspective there are no real grounds for feeling such strong attachment.

In the same way, then turn your attention towards the person you dislike and ask yourself, "On what grounds do I feel such negative emotions towards this person?" Again, this may be because he or she has done certain things towards you. But then ask yourself whether that person is likely to remain your enemy all his life. And then, if you take into account the question of many lifetimes, you will realize that the individual may have been very close to you in a past life, so his status as your enemy is merely short term. You begin to see that there are no justifiable grounds for having such extreme hatred and anger towards that person.

Finally, consider the individual in the middle, to whom you feel totally indifferent. If you raise the same kind of questions again, you will realize that the person may have very little relevance to your present life but may have been important to you in other lives in the past; and even in this lifetime, he may become important to you at some future point. So this type of visualization helps to level out the extreme fluctuating emotions that you feel towards others, and to establish a stable basis on which you can build a more balanced sense of closeness.

Gyaltsap Rinpoche has given a wonderful analogy to explain this point. He compares equanimity to fertile soil and a leveled ground. Once you have plowed a fertile field and leveled the ground, you water the soil with the moisture of love, and then you can plant the seed of compassion. If you nurture it continuously then the young shoot of *bodhichitta*, the altruistic intention, will naturally grow. I think this is a beautiful metaphor.

If we think along these lines, and question our emotions from various angles, then we come to appreciate that the extreme emotions that we tend to feel towards others, and the behaviors they generate, are perhaps unwise.

Thinking of Others as Someone Dear

Having developed equanimity, we can begin the first stage of the seven-point practice, which is cultivating the attitude of thinking of all others as being as dear to you as your mother, or father, or friend. Here, of course, the teachings take into account the idea of beginningless lifetimes, so all other sentient beings are considered to have been our mother or father or friend at one point or another. This is the way we try to relate to others and to develop a genuine sense of connection.

The reason this practice is traditionally considered so important is because, in nature, it is predominantly mothers who play the most critical role in nurturing and bringing up their offspring. In some animal species both mother and father remain together to look after their young, but in most cases it is just the mother. There are some exceptions, of course. There are some species of bird where the mother hardly participates at all in the building of the nest; it is the male that works hard to build the nest while the female just looks on and inspects the result! It then seems quite fair that the male takes greater responsibility in the nurturing process. However such cases are rare.

Butterflies offer another interesting example. The butterfly lays her eggs, and there is no possibility that she will ever meet her offspring when the caterpillars emerge, yet despite this she makes sure that the eggs are laid in a very secure area with a food supply, natural protection, and so forth. We cannot say that such animals have compassion in the sense that we understand it, but whatever the reason may be, whether it is a matter of biology or chemical processes or compassion, the fact remains that the mothers go to enormous lengths to ensure the safety and well-being of their young.

It is for these reasons that traditional Indian and Tibetan texts single out mothers as an example of how we should relate to other beings. In fact the Tibetan language has coined a special term for "dear old mother sentient beings," and the expression has become so deeply embedded in people's psyche, it has a poetic ring to it. Nowadays, whenever people raise gender issues in the context of Tibetan culture, I tell them that for me the whole idea of "mother sentient beings," and the Tibetan expression that goes with it, is a good example of how motherhood was valued in Buddhist culture. The expression for "dear old mother sentient beings," *ma gen sem chen tam che*, has a powerfully poetic and rather sentimental ring to it, whereas if you try to coin a similar expression with the male pronoun, *pa gen sem chen tam che*, it doesn't sound right at all. In fact "dear old father" in Tibetan has the derogatory connotation of someone who is rather naughty and irresponsible!

In the traditional literature, it is understood that this profound recognition of all sentient beings as being like one's mother is based upon the notion of successive lifetimes, so the whole question of rebirth and past lives comes into the picture here. The Buddhist teachings emphasize the need to understand the possibility of rebirth on the basis of understanding the nature of consciousness. The point is made, as we saw earlier, that consciousness is a phenomenon that arises due only to a previous moment of consciousness. Matter cannot become consciousness. As regards the connection between mind and matter generally, one can contribute towards the causation of the other, but in terms of an individual continuum, consciousness must be caused by a preceding moment of consciousness.

These days everybody talks about consciousness and mind, thoughts and emotions, and so on, but in Buddhism consciousness is specifically defined as "that which is of the nature of mere luminosity and knowing." It is the faculty of knowing and of basic awareness. It is fine to talk generally about these things, but I personally feel that a real understanding of what we mean by consciousness can only come from the basis of experience. I don't think that intellectual discussion or verbal description alone can convey the meaning of consciousness. In my view, an experiential understanding of consciousness or mind is invaluable.

In the Tibetan tradition we have different techniques to assist us in developing an experiential understanding of what is meant by consciousness or awareness. The Dzogchen tradition, for example, has a practice of observing the nature of mind where you begin with a sense of wonderment, then allow your thoughts to arise, and, in that neutral state, observe the activity of mind. Similarly, in the Sakya tradition of the Union of Profoundness and Clarity, one observes the nature of mind by allowing the mind to rest in its natural uncontrived state, and then observing its activity. In the Geluk and Kagyu traditions, too, there are practices of Mahamudra (the Great Seal) for identifying what is meant by mind. If you engage in such practices, and if, as a result, you have some experiential sense of what is meant by awareness, then when you try to understand the beginningless continuum of consciousness it will make some sense to you. Otherwise, the mere statement that every instance of awareness must be preceded by another instance of awareness cannot be very convincing. You need personal experience to appreciate its significance.

Reflecting on the Kindness of All Beings

The second element of the seven-point cause and effect method is reflecting upon the kindness of all beings. In your meditation, you focus on the kindness of others, especially in the context that they have been your mother in this or other lifetimes, and this naturally leads to the thought, "I must repay their kindness. I must acknowledge the profound kindness they have shown to me." Such feelings will arise naturally in someone who is honorable, ethical, and what we could call "civilized."

Once you recognize all other beings as your kind, dear mothers then naturally you will feel close to them. With this as a basis, you should cultivate love or loving-kindness, which is traditionally defined as the wish to see others enjoy happiness, and then you also develop compassion, which is the wish for others to be free of suffering. Love and compassion are two sides of the same coin.

Exchanging and Equalizing Oneself with Others

We will now turn to the other method for transforming the mind, which is exchanging and equalizing oneself with others. Here again, the first stage is the cultivation of equanimity, although the meaning of equanimity in this context is different from the one we spoke of earlier. Here, equanimity is understood as the fundamental equality of all beings, in the sense that just as you have the spontaneous wish to be happy and overcome suffering, so does every single other being, in equal measure.

Now we try to probe deeper to understand what this aspiration to be free of suffering really implies. It does not arise from a sense of self-importance, or self-congratulation; such considerations simply do not play any role here at all. This basic aspiration arises in us simply by virtue of the fact that we are conscious living beings. Together with this aspiration comes a conviction that I, as an individual, have a legitimate right to fulfill my aspiration. If we accept this, then we can relate the same principle to others and we will realize that everyone else shares this basic aspiration too. Therefore, if I as an individual have the right to fulfill my aspiration, then others, too, have an equal right to fulfill theirs. It is on these grounds that one has to recognize the fundamental equality of all beings.

Within the practice of equalizing and exchanging oneself with others, this is the equalizing stage, where we develop the understanding that we and others are fundamentally equal. The next stage involves reflecting on the shortcomings of excessively self-cherishing thoughts, and their negative consequences, as well as reflecting on the merits of developing thoughts that cherish the well-being of others.

How do we do this? We begin by comparing ourselves with others. We have accepted that there is a fundamental equality between ourselves and others in terms of our respective aspirations to be happy and overcome suffering, and we have also recognized that all beings, including ourselves, have an equal right to fulfill that aspiration. No matter how important an individual person may be, and no matter how unimportant, in a worldly sense, others may be, so far as the basic fact of wishing to be happy and overcome suffering is concerned, there is absolute equality. So what is the difference between us? The difference is really a matter of numbers. No matter how important an individual is, the interest of that individual is the interest of only one being, whereas the interest of others is the interest of an infinite number of beings.

The question is, which is more important? Simply from the numerical point of view, if we want to be fair we have to accept that the interest of others is more important than our own. Even in the mundane world we know that the issues which affect the lives of many people are generally granted greater significance than those that affect fewer people or a single individual. So, logically, one has to accept that the well-being of others is more important than one's own. To be completely rational or objective, one could say that sacrificing the interest of the many for the sake of one person is an unwise and foolish act, whereas sacrificing the interest of one individual for the benefit of an infinite number of others is more rational, if such a choice is necessary.

Now, you might think that all of this sounds fine, but at the end of the day you are "you" and others are "other." If self and others are totally independent of each other, and there is no connection whatsoever between them, then perhaps there is a case for ignoring the well-being of others and simply pursuing one's own self-interest. However, this is not the case. Self and others are not really independent; in fact, their respective interests are intertwined.

From the Buddhist point of view, even when you are unenlightened your life is so intertwined with those of others that you cannot really carve yourself out as a single isolated individual. Also, when you follow a spiritual path, many spiritual realizations depend on your interaction with others, so here again others are indispensable. Even when you have attained the highest state of enlightenment, your enlightened activities are for the benefit of others. Indeed, enlightened activity comes about spontaneously by virtue of the fact that other beings exist, so others are indispensable even at that stage. Your life and the lives of others are so interconnected that the idea of a self that is totally distinct and independent of others really does not make any sense.

Although this is the reality, it is not reflected in our behavior. Until now, regardless of reality, we have nurtured within ourselves a whole complex of self-cherishing thoughts. We believe in something that we hold very dear and we regard as precious, something that is like the core of our being; and this is accompanied by a powerful belief in our existence as an individual being with an independent reality. The belief that there is a substantially real self, and the cherishing of one's own interest at the expense of others, are the two main thoughts and emotions we have nurtured within us throughout our many lives. But what is the result of this? What benefit does it bring? We are continually suffering, we are continually experiencing negative thoughts and emotions, so our self-cherishing hasn't really got us very far. Also, if we shift our focus from ourselves to others and to the wider world, and if we turn our attention to all the crises in the world, all the difficulties and the sufferings and so on, we will see that many of these problems are direct or indirect consequences of undisciplined negative states of mind. And where do these come from? From this powerful combination of self-centeredness and the belief in our independent existence. By shifting our attention to the wider world in this way, we can begin to appreciate the immensely destructive consequences of such thinking.

These attitudes are not helpful even from one's own selfish point of view. We might ask ourselves, "What benefit do I as an individual derive from my self-centeredness, and from the belief in my existence as an independent self?" When you really think deeply, you will realize the answer is "Not very much."

In fact, these beliefs are the source of suffering and misery even for the individual. The Buddhist literature is full of discussions on this. Interestingly, about two years ago, I was at a medical conference in America, and a participating psychologist presented the findings of research he had carried out over a long period of time. One conclusion he considered almost indisputable was that there seems to be a correlation between early death, high blood pressure and heart disease on one side, and a disproportionately high use of first personal pronouns on the other ("I", "me," and "mine"). I thought this finding was very interesting. Even scientific studies seem to suggest that there is a correlation between excessive self-cherishing and damage to one's physical well-being. Incidentally, now a phrase has been coined in Tibetan, *nga rinpoche*, which means "I, the precious one." Although it sounds a bit strange, it is quite an interesting expression!

Now in contrast, if you shift your focus from yourself to others, extend your concern to others, and cultivate the thought of caring for the well-being of others, then this will have the immediate effect of opening up your life and helping you to reach out. In other words, the practice of cultivating altruism has a beneficial effect not only from the religious point of view but also from the mundane point of view, not only for long-term spiritual develop-ment but even in terms of immediate rewards. From my own per-sonal experience I can tell you that when I practice altruism and care for others, it immediately makes me calmer and more secure. So altruism brings immediate benefits.

The same applies when you cultivate the understanding that the self is not really an independently existing entity, and begin to view self instead in terms of its dependent relation to others. Although it is difficult to say that merely reflecting on this will produce a profound spiritual realization, it will at least have some effect. Your mind will be more open. Something will begin to change within you. Therefore, even in the immediate term there is definitely a positive and beneficial effect in reversing these two attitudes and moving from self-centeredness to other-centeredness, from belief in self-existence to belief in dependent origination.

To summarize, I agree with Shantideva when he writes:

What need is there to say more?
The childish work for their own benefit,
The buddhas work for the benefit of others.
Just look at the difference between them.

If I do not exchange my happiness
For the suffering of others,

I shall not attain the state of buddhahood
And even in samsara I shall have no real joy.

The source of all misery in the world
Lies in thinking of oneself;
The source of all happiness
Lies in thinking of others.

QUESTIONS

Question: If wisdom and compassion are the natural characteristics or qualities of the enlightened mind, why do we have to work so hard to cultivate them?

HHDL: Let us take a simple case like a seed. We all know that the seed has the potential to grow into a plant, as long as we put it in the right soil, fertilize it, give it moisture, maintain a certain temperature, and so on. Although we all accept that the seed has the potential within it, there is a complicated process involved, and a lot of nurturing goes into making sure that the seed grows into a fully grown plant. It is the same with us. Another reason is because the negative aspects of our mind are so ingrained.

Question: How do we distinguish between selflessness and passivity?

HHDL: I think it's important to understand that when we talk about altruism and about others' well-being, we should not imagine this means totally rejecting our own self-interest, neglecting ourselves or becoming some passive nonentity. This is a misunderstanding. In fact, the kind of altruism that focuses on the well-being of others comes about as a result of a very courageous state of mind, a very expansive attitude and a strong sense of self—so much so that the person is capable of challenging the self-cherishing self-centeredness that tends to rule our life. In order to do that, we need to have a strong sense of self and genuine courage because these tendencies seem so deeply embedded in us. This is why I normally tell people that a *bodhisattva*, a person who embodies this altruistic ideal, is, paradoxically, someone who has a very strong sense of self, because without it he or she cannot have that level of commitment and courage. So you should not think that the altruistic intention that we are talking about is a mere passive state of making pious wishes.

Question: When Your Holiness talks about controlling emotions, in the West that can sometimes mean a repression or suppression of emotions. How do we approach this practice with a lightness of mind?

HHDL: Of course it's very true that sometimes suppression
can be negative and destructive, particularly if the
feeling of resentment or anger is associated with
some painful experience in the past. Under these
circumstances, expressing emotion can be freeing.
There is a Tibetan proverb which says that if a conch
is blocked, you can clear it by blowing into it. In
Buddhism there is an understanding that certain
forms of emotion which are related to past
experiences of a painful kind are better expressed.
But generally what seems to be true, at least from
the Buddhist point of view, is that negative emotions
like anger and hatred are such that the more you
reinforce them, the more powerful they become. If
you don't recognize that their nature is destructive,
and if you relate to them as if they are natural aspects
of the psyche that simply come and go, letting the
process take its own course, then that kind of
unchecked relation to negative emotions can actually
make you more and more prone to emotional
outbursts. On the other hand, if you have a clear
recognition of their destructive potential, that very
recognition can itself have an effect so that you begin
to distance yourself from them. Gradually, their
power will begin to decrease.

Question: Why are positive thoughts and emotions to be
preferred and encouraged over negative ones? Are
they not equally impermanent and lacking in
independent existence?

HHDL: The reason why positive thoughts and emotions are
to be preferred and encouraged over negative ones is
that, although they are both equally impermanent
and equally devoid of inherent existence, the fact
remains that negative thoughts and emotions lead to
suffering and painful experiences, whereas positive
ones lead to happiness. And happiness is what we
all wish to achieve. Both happiness and pain are
changing all the time, too, so if you use that logic
there is no need to seek happiness, and no need to
make an effort to relieve ourselves of suffering! If
they are both changing from moment to moment,
then we can just lie down and wait for the change. I
don't think that this is the proper way. We should
deliberately try to implement the things that cause
happiness, and whatever causes suffering we should
deliberately try to overcome.

Question: On the spiritual path we try to abandon self-
cherishing, but in the West many people don't love
themselves, even to the point of developing chronic
depression and committing suicide. How can we deal
with these issues?

HHDL: The way I understand it, this whole concept of
          self-hatred does not mean that the person does not
          love him or herself. I actually believe that at the root
          of self-hatred there must be too much self-cherishing
          or too much attachment to oneself. One's expectation
          of oneself is so high that when that is not met there is
          intense frustration, which sets up a negative dynamic.

          I think it's very important not to misunderstand
          what is meant in the Buddhist teachings by the idea
          of overcoming our self-cherishing attitudes. We are
          not saying that a spiritual practitioner should
          completely ignore or abandon the goal of self-
          fulfillment, rather we are advising him or her to
          overcome that small-minded selfishness that makes
          us oblivious to the well-being of others and to the
          impact our actions can have on them. It is this kind
          of selfishness that is being targeted, not the kind of
          selfishness that seeks fulfillment of one's deeper
          interests. In fact, you may remember that *bodhichitta*
          is defined as the altruistic intention to become fully
          enlightened for the benefit of all sentient beings, so
          that ideal rests on an acknowledgement that the
          attainment of full enlightenment is necessary not
          only in order to be capable of benefitting others, but
          also for the perfection of our own nature. *Bodhichitta*
          therefore implies a recognition of the need to fulfill
          one's true self-interest.

In fact, if the Buddhist teachings on altruism were really suggesting that we should ignore our own self-interest and abandon it altogether, then logically this would imply that we should not work for the benefit of others either, because, according to Buddhism, one of the by-products of helping others is that you also benefit yourself. So that would mean that we should work neither for others nor for ourselves.

Also, if we look at the classical Buddhist literature on *bodhichitta*, we find for example in the *Sublime Continuum* (*Ratnagotravibhaga*) that Maitreya states that all sentient beings are perfectly equal in that they all possess the Buddha nature. This means that we all have the seed of the kindness of a buddha, and the compassion of a buddha towards all living beings, and therefore the potential for enlightenment and for perfection lies in each one of us. The point of teaching this is to instill the practitioner with a deep sense of courage and a strong sense of purpose; if that were not the case, then engaging in contemplations about the fundamental equality of all beings would be pretty pointless.

Question: Sometimes, the anger I feel has its basis in fear. When I get angry I feel more powerful, and then I am not afraid any more. How should I deal with this?

HHDL: That's very true; we all have that experience. You feel some kind of courage or power when you are angry, but actually it is a blind power. The energy of anger may not be so constructive, or it might simply be destructive: it's uncertain which way it will go. Extreme anger could eventually lead you even to taking your own life, and that is very foolish. So it is a blind energy.

If you are clearly aware of how harmful anger is, then try to look at your anger more from that viewpoint. It also depends on the object of your anger. For example, if it is directed towards an individual person then you could think about some of the positive qualities of that person, which could help to reduce your anger. On the other hand, if your anger is the result of a painful experience you have undergone, or in connection with some world crisis or disaster, then of course there are some justifiable grounds for it. Even so, if you think it through carefully, no real benefit is gained by getting angry.

Question: Your Holiness, it was edifying to read your views on the tragic situation in Kosovo. Would you mind giving us your opinion on whether you ever feel violence may be justifiable as self-defense in the case of an individual, or on a national scale in the context of defensive warfare.

HHDL: Theoretically speaking, violence and non-violence
are methods, and motivation and goals are more
important than the method itself in determining
whether an action is appropriate. So with the sincere
motivation to bring about a beneficial goal, violence
could be permissible under special circumstances.
But then on a practical level, I think one of the major
features of violence is that it is very unpredictable, so
once you commit it, it may create many
complications or side-effects that were originally
unforeseen. This is how we get violence and
counterviolence, endlessly, and a lot of suffering and
pain. I think the Kosovo situation happened exactly
like that. For this reason I think violence is better
avoided.

At a deeper level, I think the demarcation between
violence and non-violence depends very much on
motivation. If it is sincerely motivated with
compassion, then a little harsh word or harsh
physical action is essentially non-violent; with
negative motivation, such as the desire to cheat or
deceive or exploit, then even apparently friendly
words and actions are essentially violent. Motivation
is the most important factor. In this sense, violence
means any action that is motivated by hatred.

Now, that is the theoretical difference between
violence and non-violence, and if someone attacks

you and threatens your life, you have to judge their actions accordingly. Say, for instance, someone is harming you right now, you should not only defend yourself but also elicit some appropriate action from the other person, to counter their own aggression. You have to weigh up the situation. If taking countermeasures against such a threat is likely to prove insignificant, then you have to seek other means to address the problem. But if you are faced with a threat to your life, then you should run away as quickly as possible! Then again, if you're cornered and there is simply no other way out, and you happen to have a weapon, you should aim for a part of the body that will not do lasting damage to the other person, while at the same time saving you from the situation.

Whatever the circumstances, such situations are always difficult. But there is one thing which it is in our power to do. Whichever way we defend ourselves, we should not let our motivation be tinged with hatred towards the other person. We should deliberately try to act from a genuine sense of concern or sympathy.

Question: If everything is the result of cause and effect, where does free will come from?

HHDL: When we speak about cause and effect, of course, we
          are talking about a universal principle that applies to
          all things and events, both animate and inanimate.
          Within that wider context we find a further level of
          causality which concerns living beings. With human
          beings, for example, there are actions in which the
          individual engages consciously, with a certain
          intention or motivation, and these are subject to
          what is described as the karmic law of cause and
          effect. But although the law of karma is an instance
          of the general law of cause and effect, it specifically
          applies to intentional actions, actions done by
          conscious agents, so the motivation of the individual
          is an integral part of the causal process. This alone
          suggests that the individual has a very active role to
          play in determining the course of the situation.

          We have discussed the fact that we are often under
          the control of powerful negative emotions and
          thoughts, so to this extent we lack freedom, but this
          is not to say that individuals have no active part to
          play in shaping their intention. The individual's
          active role is free will. There is also another realm
          where free will plays a role. For example, even
          though an individual may have committed a karmic
          act, and have planted the seed for a particular result,
          in order for that cause to yield its result fully the
          initial cause alone is not enough—it needs

subsequent conditions to activate it. Individuals have a choice; they can ensure that these conditions do not come about.

Question: There are numerous worthy causes. How do you decide which one to devote yourself to?

HHDL: It's up to you to decide; you have to make up your own mind! I have nothing really to say. Of course, one has to relate to one's own capacity, and to what one can manage to do.

Question: There are numerous bardo beings ready to incarnate in a precious human form, but the Earth is also overpopulated. As a lay Buddhist practitioner, what would be the proper motivation when considering having a child?

HHDL: Well, it really depends very much on you. If you really want children, you have to conceive them, of course, and you also have to look after them; you have to take care of the child and ensure that it grows up well. But if you feel that this is too much and you don't want children, then you don't need to have any!

Chapter Three

TRANSFORMING THROUGH INSIGHT

Insight into the Nature of Suffering

ALONG WITH THE METHODS FOR CULTIVATING A
sense of closeness to others there is another key element for
developing compassion, and that is deepening our insight into
the nature of suffering. The Tibetan tradition maintains that
contemplation on suffering is much more effective when it is
done on the basis of one's own personal experience, and when it
is focused on oneself, because, generally, we tend to be better able
to relate to our own suffering than to that of others. This is why
two of the principal elements of the Buddhist path, compassion
and renunciation, are seen as two sides of the same coin. True
renunciation arises when one has a genuine insight into the
nature of suffering, focused upon oneself, and true compassion

arises when that focus shifts to others; so the difference lies simply in the object of focus.

Earlier, we touched briefly on the three levels of suffering according to the Buddhist teachings: the suffering of suffering, the suffering of change, and the suffering of "pervasive conditioning." I mentioned that in the context of the training in compassion and renunciation, we are talking of the third level of suffering.

So far as the first level of suffering is concerned—physical pain and other obvious sufferings—we consider that even animals have the capacity to recognize these experiences as suffering, and they are also capable of finding relief from some aspect of them, however temporary that may be. As for the suffering of change, which is the second category, this actually refers to experiences that we conventionally identify as pleasurable or happy. These are subject to the suffering of change, because the more you indulge in them, the more they lead to dissatisfaction. If these experiences were bringing some genuine lasting happiness, then the more you indulged in them the longer the experience of happiness would last, yet that is not the case. All too often what may seem like a pleasurable experience, and what may initially seem like happiness, when pursued, changes at a certain point into suffering and leads to frustration and so on. So even though conventionally it is called happiness, in another sense it has the nature of suffering. In fact, if you examine the nature of pleasurable sensations you will see that there is often an extremely relative dimension to them; we usually define an experience as pleasurable by comparison to a more intense form of suffering that has just come to an end.

What we call "pleasure" or "happiness" is more like the temporary absence of intense suffering and pain.

However, this is not the deeper meaning of suffering that we speak about in Buddhism. The suffering of change is identified as a type of suffering by many other spiritual traditions, too, and there are methods that are common to both Buddhist and non-Buddhist Indian traditions that allow the individual to recognize these experiences as suffering and to gain temporary freedom from it. These methods include various meditative techniques, the cultivation of absorptive states of mind, contemplations, and so on.

It is the third level of suffering, called "the suffering of pervasive conditioning," that we are concerned with here. The suffering of conditioning is the origin of the other two types of suffering. It is the nature of our very existence, which comes about as a result of karma, delusions, and afflictive emotions. Our very existence as unenlightened beings is said to be fundamentally unsatisfactory, or *duhkha*, that is, suffering. Through the practice of compassion and renunciation, we need to develop a genuine desire to gain freedom from this third level of suffering, but this desire can only arise if we understand the nature of suffering and its causes.

When we present the Four Noble Truths in terms of their logical evolution, it is the second truth, which is the origin of suffering, that should come first, while the first truth, that of suffering, should come second. Then the path comes third, and cessation comes fourth. However, the Buddha reversed their order when they relate to an individual's development of insight. In this context he taught suffering first, because when you understand this you will enquire into what causes it, and next into whether or not it is possible to be free of it. Only when you realize that cessation might be a possibility will you investigate the fourth truth, which is the true path or the means by which you can achieve cessation. The point here is that to have genuine renunciation it is vital to understand that true cessation is possible, based on insight into the ultimate nature of reality.

In my own personal case, I started taking a serious interest in emptiness about 30 years ago, and as a result of concerted contemplation, study, and meditation, I arrived at a point where I felt that I had a glimpse of what it must be like, although I cannot claim to have direct realization of emptiness. I told some colleagues that if ever I get to the point where I do gain true cessation, then I will take a long vacation! I said that at that stage I could afford to take a long rest, because true cessation is not just temporary relief from suffering and its causes, but their total elimination. Such is the nature of cessation that even if you come into contact with circumstances that normally give rise to negative thoughts and emotions, the basis is not there for them to arise. That is what true cessation means.

When you engage in deep contemplation on the nature of suffering, on the causes of suffering, and on the fact that there exist powerful antidotes to those causes, and when you reflect on the possibility of freedom from suffering and its causes, then you will be able to develop genuine renunciation from the depths of your heart, for you will truly aspire to gain freedom from suffering. At this stage, you will have a sense of being completely exhausted by your experience of unenlightened existence, and by the fact that you are under the domination of negative thoughts and emotions.

After you establish the aspiration to gain freedom from that kind of existence, you can shift that aspiration to others, and focus on others' experience of suffering, which is the same as your own. If you combine that with the reflections we mentioned earlier—recognizing all sentient beings as dear mothers, reflecting upon their kindness, and realizing the fundamental equality of oneself and others—then there is a real possibility for genuine compassion to arise within you. Only then will you have the genuine aspiration to be of benefit to others.

As your experience and understanding grow, so your attitude towards the Three Jewels—the Buddha, Dharma, and Sangha—will change too. The respect you have for the Buddha will become deeper, since you have a greater understanding of his teaching, the Dharma, particularly the meaning of cessation and the path leading to it. Not only is Buddha the master who gave these teachings, but he also embodied these wonderful spiritual principles. Furthermore, your admiration for the Sangha, the community of practitioners, will grow stronger and stronger since it, too, represents the Dharma. This, then, is the basis for taking refuge in the Buddha, Dharma, and Sangha.

Just as Lama Tsongkhapa says in his *In Praise of Dependent Origination*:

As you teach what you have seen yourself,
You are the unexcelled wisdom and teacher.
I pay homage to you, as you saw
and propagated Buddha's dependent origination.

If you reflect along these lines you will find that you have built a very stable foundation for practice to be successful. It is not as if you were just picking one thing at a time and blindly concentrating all your energy on that; rather you are developing an overview of the entire path, so that when you focus on a specific aspect of the practice your understanding of the wider framework enriches that practice.

Continuing on this path, you will also begin to appreciate the value of human life, how precious it is, and the fact that as human beings we are capable of reflecting on these questions and following a spiritual practice. Then you will really appreciate a point emphasized again and again by many great Tibetan masters: that we should not waste the opportunity offered to us in this life, because human life is so precious and so difficult to achieve. As life is valuable it is important to do something meaningful with it right now, since, by its very nature, it is also transient. This shows how you can bring all the elements of the various spiritual practices together so that they have a cumulative effect on your daily practice.

The point I am making is that we can train our minds by cultivating the dual aspiration to help others and to attain buddhahood for their sake. By combining these two we are able to give birth to *bodhichitta*, which is the ultimate expression of the altruistic principle, and the source of all spiritual qualities.

Reason, Faith, and Experience

There may be some doctrinal points in the Buddhist teachings whose validity may have to be accepted, at least at the initial stage, on the basis of a third person's testimony, but generally speaking, the Buddhist approach is to ground one's understanding in one's own reasoning and personal experience. Buddhism does not argue that Buddha is great because he was fully enlightened, and since the Dharma was taught by Buddha, therefore you must have faith in it. Rather, the approach we follow is to develop admiration in the Dharma first, based on an appreciation of the value of the spiritual path. This must develop through a deeper understanding of the main teachings based on personal experience and reasoning. Only then, on that basis, should one develop a deep admiration for the Buddha as the person who taught and embodied the Dharma. So the validity of Buddha as a spiritual teacher is justified by the validity of what he taught.

However, there are a few instances where the validity of the Buddha as a teacher may be used as the basis for accepting the validity of certain doctrinal points. This accords with the basic Buddhist view that there are different categories of phenomena. Many phenomena are quite evident to us. They are things or events that are accessible to us through our direct experience: we can see them, we can touch them, we can feel them, and we can prove their existence by means of our direct experience. These are called "evident" or "empirical" phenomena.

Then there is a second category of phenomena that is literally described as "slightly obscured" or "slightly hidden." Although we may not be able to perceive these directly through our senses, we can infer their existence on the basis of empirical evidence.

The third category of phenomena is described as "extremely concealed" or "extremely hidden," and these are facts of existence which remain totally hidden from us at the initial stage of our spiritual development. At this point we have simply no avenue by which we can approach them; they are not accessible either through inference or through direct perception. So, with these matters, even in Buddhism, we may initially have to accept their validity on the basis of a third person's testimony.

In this connection, I would like to address an issue which I think is common to all major world religions: the need for single-pointed faith in one's path. This is the idea that one should not try to follow two paths at once. It also includes the importance of commitment to one's own path.

This issue clearly touches on the question of exclusivism versus religious pluralism, or in other words, that of one truth versus many truths and one religion versus many religions. On the surface there does appear to be a contradiction between the following two standpoints: on the one hand, accepting there is only one truth and one true religion, and on the other accepting the possibility of many truths and many religions. However, I personally do not think there is a real contradiction here. I would suggest that from the point of view of an individual practitioner, the principle of one truth and one religion stands, but from the point of view of society or of a community of people, then the principle of many truths and many religions stands. In any society, human beings are so diverse and have so many different mentalities that I don't think there is any contradiction here.

There are, of course, many different schools of thought even within Buddhism. We could imagine someone whose philosophical inclination is to follow the Middle Way school, maintaining that the Buddha's ultimate philosophical standpoint is best represented by the Middle Way view of emptiness. Yet, at the same time, this person would acknowledge that there are numerous views included within Buddha's teachings, some of which contradict that of the Middle Way.

Likewise, a proponent of the Buddhist Mind Only school would argue that its interpretation of the non-duality of subject and object represents the highest philosophy in the Buddha's teaching, and the true middle way. This is because the Mind Only view would be more suited to that person's philosophical disposition. He might even argue that Middle Way philosophers are in fact nihilists and have gone too far.

The scriptural sources used by the Mind Only school, especially their main source, the *Sutra Unravelling the Intent of the Buddha* (*Samdhinirmocana Sutra*), are attributed to the Buddha. On reading this scripture we do not find the Buddha saying, "I say this for your benefit, to suit your mentality, but I express my own position elsewhere." There is no indication of that. The Sutra appears to state that the truths it holds represent the final reality. Indeed, it is said that teaching emptiness to those who are inclined towards Mind Only can be detrimental, because it could lead to nihilism.

So my general point is that there is enormous diversity among human beings when it comes to spiritual and philosophical inclinations. Another example is that, for some people, the concept of a divine Creator is very powerful, inspiring, and effective as the core of their spiritual belief. The idea of having just one life, just this life, and of being created by a Creator, directly, can bring the feeling of having a very close relationship with Him. This sense of intimacy and direct connection with the Creator is very powerful, so it can form a sound basis for the wish to lead an ethical life. The closer one feels to the Creator, the greater one's effort will be to live according to His wishes.

And again, even amongst theists there is great diversity. Christians have the concept of a Trinity, but Muslims have no such notion and teach a much more direct link with the Creator. This suggests that theists themselves have many different spiritual inclinations. The key to this question, I think, is that whatever you find most effective, whatever is most suited to your temperament and spiritual inclination, is the path for you.

Insight into the Ultimate Nature of Reality

The idea of no-self, that is, the rejection of self-existence, is common to all Buddhist schools. The reason so much emphasis is placed on the rejection of an eternal soul or self in the Buddhist teachings is that much of our confusion and suffering is seen to arise from a false sense of self, and in particular from a belief in some kind of eternal independently existing self at the core of our being. An indispensable element of the path that leads to overcoming these afflictions is therefore to realize the non-existence of such a self.

All Buddhist schools accept the no-self doctrine, but some schools take it further than others and assert that we should not only reject the independent and solid existence of the self, but we should extend the same reasoning to all phenomena, that is, to the objects of our experience. Just as the subject is devoid of any independent discrete existence, similarly the field of experience, or phenomena, must be seen in the same way. So these schools accept the no-self doctrine in relation to both persons and phenomena.

There are two schools which assert this, namely the Mind Only (Cittamatra) school and the Middle Way (Madhyamaka) school of Buddhism. The Middle Way school generally rejects any notion of phenomena as possessing an intrinsic nature, existence or identity. When I spoke in London on a previous occasion, I discussed the Middle Way philosophy of no-self, so today I feel that it is perhaps more appropriate to discuss the Mind Only school's understanding of the nature of reality.

The View of the Mind Only School

The Mind Only school takes issue with the Middle Way school's characterization of no-self as the absence of intrinsic existence or intrinsic identity. Adherents of this school object on the grounds that if one negates these, then the principle of dependent origination, which is so fundamental to Buddhist philosophy, becomes untenable. If we are to maintain a coherent understanding of dependent origination, in their view, we must accept that there are things which interact with each other and which depend upon each other. So they argue that things must have intrinsic existence or an intrinsic nature.

Given their opposition to the Madhyamakas' wholesale rejection of intrinsic existence, the Mind Only school must find a way of interpreting passages in the *Perfection of Wisdom* (*Prajñaparamita*) *Sutras* which seem to support the Madhyamaka view. This is done by way of their theory of the Three Natures. According to this, the absence of intrinsic identity must be understood differently in different contexts. There is a nature of phenomena that is merely imputed by our minds, and that is therefore a mere construct of our thinking. This, according to the Mind Only school, is the imputed nature (*parakalpita*). This imputed nature is said to be devoid of intrinsic characteristics. Second, there is the dependent nature (*paratantra*) of phenomena, which do possess an intrinsic nature but are devoid of independent production. This means that they do not come into being on their own; rather, they do so as a result of other causes and conditions. The third nature is called the ultimate nature (*parinispanna*), which is described as "emptiness." This is said to be devoid of absolute identity.

The Mind Only school argues that these three natures are universal, which means, by definition, that they extend to all phenomena. Each phenomenon possesses a dependent nature, an imputed nature, and an ultimate nature. Moreover, these three are intimately interconnected—the dependent nature is the basis upon which we project our mental constructs; the independent reality that we tend to conceive in relation to dependent things is the imputed nature; and the absence of reality of that construct is the ultimate reality. So the dependent nature is the basis, imputed nature the construct that we project, and ultimate reality is the emptiness of this construct.

The Mind Only school characterizes this ultimate nature or emptiness in two different ways. In one way, it is described as the non-duality of subject and object. It is argued that in the final analysis the perceiver and the perceived, the subject and object, are non-dual, and that it is our imagination that constructs the separation of the two. Alternatively, they argue that in our normal perception, we tend to view objects as if they have some kind of objective criteria which make them the referents of our language and concepts. But this is, however, not the case.

For example, we refer to an object with a particular term and label it accordingly, but the object itself does not exist for its part, as the referent of that label. Rather, it is our language and thought processes that link a conceptual term with an object. The Mind

Only school argues that the way we relate words and concepts to objects is merely relative, conditional or provisional, and yet we do not behave as though this were the case. If we are asked, "What does the word 'body' mean?" we would instinctively point to a physical body and say, "That's a body." Somehow we believe that there is something objectively real about the body that makes it the referent of the term "body" and its associated concepts. However, according to the Mind Only school this is not the case. The reference of the term "body" to the object "body" arises as part of a complex system of convention. If there were something objectively real about the relationship between the term and the object, then it is argued that we should be able to have the idea that "This is a body" even before we have applied our labeling thought. Despite this, we normally behave as if things themselves somehow carry a kind of absolute relation to the words that designate them, and as if things have an independent objective reality that renders it appropriate for us to refer to them with these terms.

The Mind Only school puts forward a way of approaching the deeper nature of reality through a process of enquiry into the nature of names and terms, the referents of those terms, the nature of phenomena, and the specific characteristics of phenomena. This approach is known as the Four Searchings, or Enquiry through the Four Avenues. It gives rise to insight into these four aspects of phenomena, namely the term, the referent, the nature, and the characteristics. This is then said to lead to an understanding of their ultimate nature, the non-duality of the perceived object and the perceiving subject.

Although in our naïve world view, we tend to believe that things really exist objectively outside us, as we normally perceive them, in reality the perception of an object and the actual thing itself are not separate. They are said to be two aspects of the same phenomenon. Thus, this school maintains that what we perceive as the external reality of matter is simply a projection of our mind. In reality, the perceiver and the perceived are simultaneous; they share the same reality, and both arise from the same source.

The Mind Only school accounts for the complexity of perception by breaking the process down into several aspects. When we perceive an object, like a form, there is the element of seeing something as something, like seeing a blue object as a blue object. Then within that perception, there is also the perception that the blue object exists as the true referent of the term "blue." There is another aspect of perception whereby we also believe that this blue object exists as the referent of the term "blue" objectively, of its own accord. And finally, there is a perception of that blue object as something that is independent and separate from perception itself.

The Mind Only school then explains the dynamics of these different aspects of perception by attributing different propensities to us. It argues that the fact that we perceive a blue object as blue is due to our being habituated to repeated perceptions of blue things. The aspect of our seeing blue as the referent of the term "blue" is said to be due to our habituation to language and conventions; and our perception that the blue object is not only a referent of the term "blue" but also exists by itself, objectively, is said to be the imprint of our tendency to grasp at the idea of independent existence (in this case, the existence of blue). Lastly, the aspect of our perception whereby we tend to take the blue object as being independent of the perception we have of it is said to be the imprint of another propensity described as "the propensity of unenlightened existence." Of these four imprints, the first two are considered valid, and their corresponding aspects of perception are valid, too; but the last two imprints and the perceptions that go with them are said to be deluded.

Ultimately, the standpoint of the Mind Only school is that the subject, the perceived object, and the faculty of apperception (a reflexive quality of consciousness) are all different aspects of the same phenomenon. This is how they establish their understanding of the ultimate nature of reality as the non-duality of subject and object. There is therefore a major difference in the understanding of ultimate reality between the Mind Only and other Mahayana schools. But as far as their understanding of the overall framework of the spiritual path is concerned, there is no difference between the schools.

For someone who is interested in Buddhist philosophy I think it is very important to understand the Mind Only school's view of ultimate reality. We should take their objections against the Middle Way school seriously. Their contention is that if, like the Madhyamakas, one rejects any notion of intrinsic existence, identity or nature, then one is susceptible to nihilism. It follows that a true understanding of the Middle Way philosophy of emptiness is only possible if we can distinguish between the negation of the intrinsic existence and identity of things, and the rejection of existence *per se*. In other words, we must be able to respond to the criticism of the Mind Only school and defend the Middle Way's rejection of intrinsic being while not denying existence altogether.

In the twenty-sixth chapter of his *Fundamental Wisdom of the Middle Way* (*Mulamadhyamakakarika*), in which he examines the Twelve Links of dependent origination, the Madhyamaka master Nagarjuna takes great pains to defend the Middle Way's rejection of intrinsic existence on the grounds that it is not nihilistic. There is thus a great difference between emptiness and mere nothingness, and between the rejection of intrinsic existence and the rejection of existence altogether.

QUESTIONS

Question: I can accept that as a practice and a long-term goal, we can eliminate afflictive emotions through insight into emptiness. But when one is in the midst of anger, how can one work with it there and then?

HHDL: This depends very much on the individual. In the case of a practitioner who has a profound experience of *bodhichitta*, a sense of renunciation of mundane matters, and some understanding of emptiness, then the instances of strong negative emotions like anger and hatred will be quite rare. Even when they do arise, such a person is capable of instantly recollecting the teaching and connecting with his or her spiritual realization, which can immediately diffuse the intensity of the negative emotion.

However, for those who, like myself, do not have such profound realizations, the best method is to try to ensure that you do not find yourself in situations or circumstances that could give rise to powerful negative emotions. It is generally said that for beginners, prevention is far more effective than confrontation, and I think this is very true. From experience you can get a sense of the kind of circumstances that can lead you to outbursts of strong negative emotions, and you can do your utmost to avoid these. However, when strong negative emotions like anger or hatred do actually arise in you, you might find a way of dealing with them if they have not fully exploded, but if they have, there may not really be much you can do. In that case, perhaps the best thing is just to scream your head off!

When I was a child in the Norbulingka Summer Palace in Tibet, the palace sweepers used to tell me that whenever I got angry with my playmates I should bite my fists. Looking back now, it does seem to be quite sensible advice, because if you think about it, the likelihood is that the more intense the anger, the more forcefully you are going to bite yourself. This will really wake you up and remind you not to be so angry, because you yourself will experience the pain of being bitten. Also, the pain will have the immediate effect of diverting your mind away from your anger.

Question: Your Holiness, I want so much to be a better, kinder human being, to be compassionate, and to get rid of all my negative thoughts and actions, but the harder I try to work towards this, the more mistakes I make, the more I seem to slip back. It feels like walking through sludge. Do you have any advice?

HHDL: I personally feel that this is an indication that you have taken the advice very seriously. In fact, the situation is very similar to when someone begins to meditate for the first time. When you pause to sit down, reflect, and try to meditate, you begin to see that your thoughts are so changeable, and there is so much distraction in your mind, it is as though you have become more distracted by meditating. Actually, that is a good sign, a sign that you are beginning to make progress.

Now, as I explained, transforming the mind is not easy. It takes time, so you should not lose courage and interest, you should just carry on. It is helpful to think in terms not just of a few weeks or a few months or a few years, but of life after life—a thousand lives, a million lives, trillions of lives, aeons, limitless aeons. That is the Buddhist way of thinking.

Whenever I feel a certain frustration myself, or too much sadness, then I remember that beautiful verse: "As long as space endures, as long as sentient beings remain, until then, may I too remain and dispel the miseries of the world." I repeat that verse, think about it and meditate on it, and instantly my mental frustration disappears. So you need more determination; irrespective of the time it takes to change, you need to develop that kind of determination and then things become much easier. If you want immediate results, then things are more difficult. That's my experience. If you find something useful in it, then try to follow it. If you find it is meaningless, then I don't know what to say, I have no other advice to give you.

Chapter Four

THE EIGHT VERSES ON
TRANSFORMING THE MIND

UNTIL NOW, WE HAVE TALKED ABOUT THE BASIS
that makes spiritual transformation possible, and about the need
for training the mind. The most essential point is the development of *bodhichitta*, the altruistic intention to attain enlightenment for the sake of all sentient beings, which arises from training
in the two aspirations. As a means to enhance our practice it is
advised that we should constantly apply it in our daily life, and to
our behavior as a whole—physical, verbal, and mental. Verbal
action includes reading texts like *The Eight Verses on Transforming
the Mind*, which is presented here (see Appendix I) as an aid to
constantly remind you of the importance of undertaking this
kind of contemplation.

Let us situate the practice of *bodhichitta* within the context of
Tibetan Buddhism as a whole. Tibetan Buddhism can be described

as the most comprehensive system of Buddhism in the sense that it contains elements of all the aspects of the Buddha's teachings, including Vajrayana. The teachings of the Four Noble Truths form the core of the non-Mahayana teachings, and are really the foundation of the Buddhist path. Together with the training in morality, the Four Noble Truths also serve as the basis for the practice of *bodhichitta*.

The development of *bodhichitta* is the core of the Buddha's teaching, and the main path. Once the development of *bodhichitta* has taken place, the practitioner endeavors to apply the altruistic principle throughout his or her life. This leads to what are known as the "bodhisattva ideals," including the "six perfections"—the perfections of generosity, morality, patience, enthusiasm, meditation or concentration, and wisdom. Of these six, the last two are perhaps the most important because it is in the context of the perfection of concentration and insight that the Vajrayana methods are introduced. We can consider the Vajrayana teachings as more refined methods for realizing the perfection of concentration and wisdom. The highest practice for perfecting these, from the Tibetan Buddhist point of view, is said to be the Highest Yoga Tantra (*anuttarayoga tantra*) where a detailed explanation of the subtle levels of consciousness can be found.

The point I wish to make here is that the practice of compassion is at the heart of the entire path. All other practices are either preliminary to it, or a foundation for it, or they are subsequent applications of this core practice. I would also like to point out that there is a consensus between all Buddhist schools on this, in both Mahayana and non-Mahayana traditions. So compassion lies at the root of all the Buddha's teaching, but it is within the bodhisattva ideal that we find special emphasis on the concerted development of compassion by means of cultivating *bodhichitta*.

THE EIGHT VERSES

With a determination to achieve the highest aim
For the benefit of all sentient beings
Which surpasses even the wish-fulfilling gem,
May I hold them dear at all times.

The first verse begins in Tibetan with a reference to self, and we touched briefly on the question of self in Chapter 1. We will now pursue this issue further.

The analysis of the nature and existence of self is really critical for an understanding of the Buddhist path. We could say that there are two main camps on this issue within Buddhism. On the one hand there are Buddhist schools which, although they reject the self as an eternal principle or eternal soul, argue that a self, or person, or individual, must be identified in relation to the mind–body aggregates. For instance, some schools posit the person as the total collection of the five aggregates. Others argue that it is the mental consciousness that is the real person or self. The Indian master Bhavaviveka, for example, identified the sixth mental consciousness[1] as the person in the final analysis. However, other schools, such as the Mind Only school, are not satisfied with the identification of the person with a mental consciousness. They posit a separate faculty called the "foundational consciousness" (*alaya vijñana*) which is said to remain constant, ever-present, and continuous. It is also said to be neutral, and acts as a repository for the many propensities that exist in our mind-stream.

So this group of Buddhist schools attempts to identify the self objectively with the mind–body complex. Why did the Mind Only school feel the need to posit a foundational consciousness separate from our general mental consciousness? They found there are instances in life, particularly for a highly evolved meditator in total equipoise on emptiness, when no aspect of the meditator's consciousness is polluted. Yet he or she has not attained full enlightenment, so the mental pollutants and their imprints must still reside somewhere. This is why they felt the need to posit a separate faculty called the foundational consciousness, which is by its very nature a neutral state.

On the other side, there is a school of Buddhism called Prasangika Madhyamaka which rejects any need to posit the self objectively as an inherently existing entity. They argue that we cannot posit either the self or things and events as possessing

---

[1] Classical Buddhism distinguishes six consciousnesses: the visual consciousness, the auditory consciousness, the olfactory consciousness, the tactile consciousness, the consciousness of taste, and the mental consciousness.

independent objective reality. One must understand the existence of the self or person as a construct in relation to the mind–body complex, something that is imputed on the basis of mind and body but that has no independent existence or inherent identity.

From the second and more profound point of view, we say that the self is a designation imputed to the complex of mind–body aggregates. The Prasangikas maintain that the nature of self is such that when you actually begin to search for its real existence on the basis of its alleged physical and mental constituents, you cannot find anything that can be identified as the real "self." Prasangika Madhyamaka subjects the notion of self to what is called the "seven-point analysis"[2] and finally states that since a self or person cannot be found when we analyze our body and mind, we should not conclude that it does not exist at all, but rather that it exists as a designation.

One of the implications that they draw from this approach is that we should not engage in excessive analysis, and try to posit a metaphysical reality to self, rather we should accept the reality of the self or person on the basis of general convention, and should not investigate beyond that. So when you begin to appreciate that the reality of self can be accepted as valid only at the level of popular convention, and at the level of linguistic usage, then you realize that one cannot posit any objective inherent

---

[2] This analysis investigates seven possibilities one by one. They are: the self is not identical to its parts, the self is not other than its parts, the self is not the base of its parts, the self does not inherently depend on its parts, the self does not inherently possess parts, the self is not the shape of its parts, and the self is not the composite of its parts.

reality to it. Furthermore, you also come to realize that the self has no independent identity of its own, and does not exist inherently. Persons do not exist in and of themselves, but merely within the context of language and of the understanding that prevails in the transactional world. This analysis is a very skillful way to gain insight into the emptiness of persons.

The Prasangikas are suggesting that persons are somehow real in name and concept, but not in objective reality. However, this concept is slightly different from the notion of abstract entities held by other Buddhist schools which likewise say that entities are real only in name and concept. It is important not to be confused by this. Although the same term may be used by different Buddhist schools, its meaning may change in different contexts and when used by different philosophers. This is true, for instance, of the word for "intrinsic nature," *svabhava*. We sometimes find the word used in the writings of Prasangika Madhyamaka philosophers who reject the notion of inherent existence. The mere fact that they use the word in some contexts does not mean that they accept inherent existence. It is therefore important to be sensitive to the specific context in which a word appears.

When we refer to the "I" in the context of the *Eight Verses*, therefore, we should not see it as some form of objectively real or substantially existent self. We should always bear in mind that the self is understood as the conventional person.

In this verse you are making the aspiration to hold all other sentient beings as supremely dear to you, because they are the basis upon which you can achieve the highest goal, which is the welfare of sentient beings. This goal surpasses even the legendary wish-fulfilling jewel, because however precious such a jewel may be, it cannot provide the highest spiritual attainment. There is also a reference here to the kindness of all other beings, and we spoke of the meaning of this earlier. For a Mahayana practitioner especially, it is due to other sentient beings that you can develop great compassion, the highest spiritual principle, and it is thanks to other sentient beings that you can develop *bodhichitta*, the altruistic intention. So it is on the basis of your interaction with others that you can attain the highest spiritual realizations. From that point of view, the kindness of others is very profound.

We find a similar principle at work in other fields of spiritual practice such as the "three higher trainings"—the trainings in morality, meditation and insight. The role played by others is very important in these trainings, right from the start. Let's take, for example, the higher training in morality. The essence of the Buddhist training in morality is the ethics of restraint, that is, refraining from harming others; and the core practice is refraining from the ten negative actions, the first of which is not to kill. So the very first practice of ethical discipline, not to kill, is directly connected with the value of the role played by others. Furthermore, according to Buddhism some of the positive qualities that we desire in life, such as longevity, an attractive appearance, being wealthy, having all one needs, and so on, these are all said to be the karmic results of your interaction with others. Longevity, for instance, is said to be an effect of the ethical practice of refraining from killing; being physically attractive is said to result from being patient with others; being well-provided for is seen as the result of having been generous towards others in one's previous life; and so on. So even the mundane advantages that we strive for are considered to be the fruit of our interaction with others.

When we talk of cultivating the thought of holding others as supremely dear, it is important to understand that we are not cultivating the kind of pity that we sometimes feel towards someone who is less fortunate than ourselves. With pity, there can be a tendency to look down upon the object of our compassion, and to feel a sense of superiority. Holding others dear is in fact the reverse of this. In this practice, by recognizing the kindness of others and how indispensable they are for our own spiritual progress, we appreciate their tremendous importance and significance, and therefore we naturally accord them a higher status in our minds. It is because we think of them in this way that we are able to relate to them as dear, and as worthy of our respect and affection. Because of this, the next verse reads:

Whenever I interact with someone,
May I view myself as the lowest amongst all,
And, from the very depths of my heart,
Respectfully hold others as superior.

This verse suggests the kind of attitude that I have just described. The idea of seeing oneself as lower than others should not be misconstrued as a way of neglecting ourselves, ignoring our needs, or feeling that we are a hopeless case. Rather, as I explained earlier, it stems from a courageous state of mind where you are able to relate to others, fully aware of what ability you have to help. So please do not misunderstand this point. What is being suggested here is the need for genuine humility.

I would like to tell a story to illustrate this. There was a great Dzogchen master about two or three generations ago called Dza Paltrul Rinpoche. Not only was he a great master but he had a large following, and he would often give teachings to thousands of students. But he was also a meditator, so occasionally he would disappear to do a retreat somewhere, and his students would have to run around to search for him. During one of these breaks he was on a pilgrimage, and he stayed for a couple of days with a family, like many Tibetan pilgrims did; they would seek shelter with a family on the road and do some chores in return for food. So Dza Paltrul Rinpoche did various chores for the family, including emptying the mother's potty, which he did on a regular basis.

Eventually some of his students arrived in that region, and heard that Dza Paltrul Rinpoche was somewhere around, and a number of monks finally reached this household and approached the mother of the house. "Do you know where Dza Paltrul Rinpoche is?" they asked. "I don't know of any Dza Paltrul Rinpoche around here," she replied. The monks then described him to her, and added, "We heard he was living in your house as a pilgrim." "Oh," she cried, "*that* is Dza Paltrul Rinpoche!" Apparently, just at that moment, Dza Paltrul Rinpoche had gone to empty her potty. The mother was so horrified that she ran away!

What this story tells us is that even in a great lama like Dza Pal-trul Rinpoche, who had a following of thousands, and who was used to giving teachings from a high throne, surrounded by many monks, and so on, there was a genuine humility. He had no hesitation when it came to doing a chore like emptying the potty of an elderly lady.

There are particular ways in which one can practice viewing oneself as lower than others. To take a simple example, we all know from experience that when we focus on a particular object or individual, according to the angle from which we view it, we will have a different perspective. This is, in fact, the nature of thought. Thoughts are capable of selecting only isolated characteristics of a given object at a particular time, human thought is not capable of comprehensively viewing something in its entirety. The nature of thought is to be selective. When you realize this, you can view yourself as lower than others from a certain point of view, even in comparison to a tiny insect.

Let's say that I compare myself to an insect. I am a follower of the Buddha, and a human being equipped with the capacity to think and, supposedly, to be able to judge between right and wrong. I am also supposed to have some knowledge of the fundamental teachings of the Buddha, and theoretically I am committed to these practices. Yet when I find certain negative tendencies arising in me, or when I carry out negative actions on the basis of these impulses, then from that point of view there is certainly a case to be made that I am in some ways inferior to the insect. After all, an insect is not able to judge between right and wrong in the way humans can, it has no capacity to think in a long-term way and is unable to understand the intricacies of spiritual teachings, so from the Buddhist point of view, whatever an insect does is the result of habituation and karma. By comparison, human beings have the ability to determine what they do. If, despite this, we act negatively then it could be argued that we are inferior to that innocent insect! So when you think along these lines, there are genuine grounds for seeing ourselves as inferior to all other sentient beings.

The third verse reads:

In all my deeds may I probe into my mind,
And as soon as mental and emotional afflictions arise—
As they endanger myself and others—
May I strongly confront them and avert them.

This indicates that although all of us, as spiritual practitioners, wish to overcome our negative impulses, thoughts and emotions, owing to our long habituation to negative tendencies, and to our lack of diligence in applying the necessary antidotes to them, afflictive emotions and thoughts do occur in us spontaneously and quite powerfully. Such is their force, in fact, that we are often driven by these negative tendencies. This verse suggests we should be aware of this fact so that we remain alert. We should constantly check ourselves and take note when negative tendencies arise in us, so that we can catch them as they arise. If we do this then we will not give in to them; we will be able to remain on our guard and keep a certain distance from them. In this way we won't reinforce them, and we will be spared from undergoing an explosion of strong emotion and the negative words and actions to which that leads.

But generally, this is not what happens. Even if we know that negative emotions are destructive, if they are not very intense we tend to think, "Oh, maybe this one is OK." We tend to treat them rather casually. The problem is that the longer you are accustomed to the afflictions within you, the more prone you become to their re-occurring, and then the greater your propensity will be to give in to them. This is how negativity perpetuates itself. So it is important to be mindful, as the text urges, so that whenever afflictive emotions arise you are able to confront them and avert them immediately.

Earlier, I pointed out that the Buddhist teaching must be understood in relation to the goal of attaining freedom from suffering, and that the heart of the Buddhist spiritual practice is therefore to work with negative tendencies. It is very important, especially for a Buddhist practitioner, to constantly check oneself in daily life, to check one's thoughts and feelings even, if possible, during one's dreams. As you train yourself in the application of mindfulness, gradually you will be able to apply it more and more regularly, and its effectiveness as a tool will increase.

The next verse reads:

When I see beings of unpleasant character
Oppressed by strong negativity and suffering,

May I hold them dear—for they are rare to find—
As if I have discovered a jewel treasure!

This verse refers to the special case of relating to people who are socially marginalized, perhaps because of their behavior, their appearance, their destitution, or on account of some illness. Whoever practices *bodhichitta* must take special care of these people, as if, on meeting them, you have found a real treasure. Instead of feeling repulsed, a true practitioner of these altruistic principles should engage and take on the challenge of relating. In fact, the way we interact with people of this kind could give a great impetus to our spiritual practice.

In this context, I would like to point out the great example set by many Christian brothers and sisters who engage in the humanitarian and caring professions especially directed to marginalized members of society. One such example in our times was the late Mother Teresa, who dedicated her life to caring for the destitute. She exemplified the ideal that is described in this verse.

It is on account of this important point that when I meet members of Buddhist centers in various parts of the world, I often point out to them that it is not sufficient for a Buddhist center simply to have programs of teaching or meditation. There are, of course, very impressive Buddhist centers, and some retreat centers, where the Western monks have been trained so well that they are capable of playing the clarinet in the traditional Tibetan way! But I also emphasize to them the need to bring the social and caring dimension into their program of activities, so that the principles presented in the Buddhist teachings can make a contribution to society.

I am glad to say that I've heard that some Buddhist centers are beginning to apply Buddhist principles socially. For example, I believe that in Australia there are Buddhist centers which are establishing hospices and helping dying people, and caring for patients with Aids. I have also heard of Buddhist centers involved in some form of spiritual education in prisons, where they give talks and offer counseling. I think these are great examples. It is of course deeply unfortunate when such people, particularly prisoners, feel rejected by society. Not only is it deeply painful for them, but also, from a broader point of view, it is a loss for society. We are not providing the opportunity for these people to make a constructive social contribution when they actually have the potential to do so. I therefore think it is important for society as a whole not to reject such individuals, but to embrace them and acknowledge the potential contribution they can make. In this way they will feel they have a place in society, and will begin to think that they might perhaps have something to offer.

The next verse reads:

When others, out of jealousy
Treat me wrongly with abuse, slander, and scorn,
May I take upon myself the defeat
And offer to others the victory.

The point that is made here is that when others provoke you, perhaps for no reason or unjustly, instead of reacting in a negative way, as a true practitioner of altruism you should be able to be tolerant towards them. You should remain unperturbed by such treatment. In the next verse we learn that not only should we be tolerant of such people, but in fact we should view them as our spiritual teachers. It reads:

When someone whom I have helped,
Or in whom I have placed great hopes,
Mistreats me in extremely hurtful ways,
May I regard him still as my precious teacher.

In Shantideva's *Guide to the Bodhisattva's Way of Life*, there is an extensive discussion of how we can develop this kind of attitude, and how we can actually learn to see those who perpetrate harm on us as objects of spiritual learning. And also, in the third chapter of Chandrakirti's *Entry to the Middle Way*, there are profoundly inspiring and effective teachings on the cultivation of patience and tolerance.

The seventh verse summarizes all the practices that we have been discussing. It reads:

In brief, may I offer benefit and joy
To all my mothers, both directly and indirectly,
May I quietly take upon myself
All hurts and pains of my mothers.

This verse presents a specific Buddhist practice known as "the practice of giving and taking" (*tong len*), and it is by means of the visualization of giving and taking that we practice equalizing and exchanging ourselves with others.

"Exchanging ourselves with others" should not be taken in the literal sense of turning oneself into the other and the other into oneself. This is impossible anyway. What is meant here is a reversal of the attitudes one normally has towards oneself and others. We tend to relate to this so-called "self" as a precious core at the center of our being, something that is really worth taking care of, to the extent that we are willing to overlook the well-being of others. In contrast, our attitude towards others often resembles indifference; at best we may have some concern for them, but even this may simply remain at the level of a feeling or an emotion. On the whole we are indifferent towards others' well-being and do not take it seriously. So the point of this particular practice is to reverse this attitude so that we reduce the intensity of our grasping and the attachment we have to ourselves, and endeavor to consider the well-being of others as significant and important.

When approaching Buddhist practices of this kind, where there is a suggestion that we should take harm and suffering upon ourselves, I think it is vital to consider them carefully and appreciate them in their proper context. What is actually being suggested here is that if, in the process of following your spiritual path and learning to think about the welfare of others, you are led to take on certain hardships or even suffering, then you should be totally prepared for this. The texts do not imply that you should hate yourself, or be harsh on yourself, or somehow wish misery upon yourself in a masochistic way. It is important to know that this is not the meaning.

Another example we should not misinterpret is the verse in a famous Tibetan text which reads, "May I have the courage if necessary to spend aeons and aeons, innumerable lifetimes, even in the deepest hell realm." The point that is being made here is that the level of your courage should be such that if this is required of you as part of the process of working for others' well-being, then you should have the willingness and commitment to accept it.

A correct understanding of these passages is very important, because otherwise you may use them to reinforce any feelings of self-hatred, thinking that if the self is the embodiment of self-centeredness, one should banish oneself into oblivion. Do not forget that ultimately the motivation behind wishing to follow a spiritual path is to attain supreme happiness, so just as one seeks happiness for oneself one is also seeking happiness for others. Even from a practical point of view, for someone to develop genuine compassion towards others, first he or she must have a basis upon which to cultivate compassion, and that basis is the ability to connect to one's own feelings and to care for one's own welfare. If one is not capable of doing that, how can one reach out to others and feel concern for them? Caring for others requires caring for oneself.

The practice of *tong len*, giving and taking, encapsulates the practices of loving-kindness and compassion: the practice of giving emphasizes the practice of loving-kindness, whereas the practice of taking emphasizes the practice of compassion.

Shantideva suggests an interesting way of doing this practice in his *Guide to the Bodhisattva's Way of Life*. It is a visualization to help us appreciate the shortcomings of self-centeredness, and provide us with methods to confront it. On one side you visualize your own normal self, the self that is totally impervious to others' well-being and an embodiment of self-centeredness. This is the self that only cares about its own well-being, to the extent that it is often willing to exploit others quite arrogantly to reach its own ends. Then, on the other side, you visualize a group of beings who are suffering, with no protection and no refuge. You can focus your attention on specific individuals if you wish. For example, if you wish to visualize someone you know well and care about, and who is suffering, then you can take that person as a specific object of your visualization and do the entire practice of giving and taking in relation to him or her. Thirdly, you view yourself as a neutral third person or impartial observer, who tries to assess whose interest is more important here. Isolating yourself in the position of neutral observer makes it easier for you to see the limitations of self-centeredness, and realize how much fairer and more rational it is to concern yourself with the welfare of other sentient beings.

As a result of this visualization, you slowly begin to feel an affinity with others and a deep empathy with their suffering, and at this point you can begin the actual meditation of giving and taking.

In order to carry out the meditation on taking, it is often quite helpful to do another visualization. First, you focus your attention on suffering beings, and try to develop and intensify your compassion towards them, to the point where you feel that their suffering is almost unbearable. At the same time, however, you realize that there is not much you can do to help them in a practical sense. So in order to train yourself to become more effective, with a compassionate motivation you visualize taking upon yourself their suffering, the causes of their suffering, their negative thoughts and emotions, and so forth. You can do this by imagining all their suffering and negativity as a stream of dark smoke, and you visualize this smoke dissolving into you.

In the context of this practice you can also visualize sharing your own positive qualities with others. You can think of any meritorious actions that you have done, any positive potential that may lie in you, and also any spiritual knowledge or insight that you may have attained. You send them out to other sentient beings, so that they too can enjoy their benefits. You can do this by imagining your qualities in the form of either a bright light or a whitish stream of light, which penetrates other beings and is absorbed into them. This is how to practice the visualization of taking and giving.

Of course, this kind of meditation will not have a material effect on others because it is a visualization, but what it can do is help increase your concern for others and your empathy with their suffering, while also helping to reduce the power of your self-centeredness. These are the benefits of the practice.

This is how you train your mind to cultivate the altruistic aspiration to help other sentient beings. When this arises together with the aspiration to attain full enlightenment, then you have realized *bodhichitta*, that is, the altruistic intention to become fully enlightened for the sake of all sentient beings.

In the final verse, we read:

May all this remain undefiled
By the stains of the eight mundane concerns;
And may I, recognizing all things as illusion,
Devoid of clinging, be released from bondage.

The first two lines of this verse are very critical for a genuine practitioner. The eight mundane concerns are attitudes that tend to dominate our lives generally. They are: becoming elated when someone praises you, becoming depressed when someone insults or belittles you, feeling happy when you experience success, being depressed when you experience failure, being joyful when you acquire wealth, feeling dispirited when you become poor, being pleased when you have fame, and feeling depressed when you lack recognition.

A true practitioner should ensure that his or her cultivation of altruism is not defiled by these thoughts. For example, if, as I am giving this talk, I have even the slightest thought in the back of my mind that I hope people admire me, then that indicates that my motivation is defiled by mundane considerations, or what the Tibetans call the "eight mundane concerns." It is very important to check oneself and ensure that is not the case. Similarly, a practitioner may apply altruistic ideals in his daily life, but if all of a sudden he feels proud about it and thinks, "Ah, I'm a great practitioner," immediately the eight mundane concerns defile his practice. The same applies if a practitioner thinks, "I hope people admire what I'm doing," expecting to receive praise for the great effort he is making. All these are mundane concerns that spoil one's practice, and it is important to ensure that this does not happen so we keep our practice pure.

As you can see, the instructions that you can find in the *lo-jong* teachings on transforming the mind are very powerful. They really make you think. For example there is a passage which says:

> *May I be gladdened when someone belittles me, and may I not take pleasure when someone praises me. If I do take pleasure in praise then it immediately increases my arrogance, pride, and conceit; whereas if I take pleasure in criticism, then at least it will open my eyes to my own shortcomings.*

This is indeed a powerful sentiment.

Up to this point we have discussed all the practices that are related to the cultivation of what is known as "conventional *bodhichitta*," the altruistic intention to become fully enlightened for the benefit of all sentient beings. Now, the last two lines of the *Eight Verses* relate to the practice of cultivating what is known as "ultimate *bodhichitta*," which refers to the development of insight into the ultimate nature of reality.

Although the generation of wisdom is part of the bodhisattva ideal, as embodied in the six perfections,[3] generally speaking, as

---

[3]   These are the perfections of generosity, discipline, patience, effort, meditation, and wisdom.

we saw earlier, there are two main aspects to the Buddhist path—method and wisdom. Both are included in the definition of enlightenment, which is the non-duality of perfected form and perfected wisdom. The practice of wisdom or insight correlates with the perfection of wisdom, while the practice of skillful means or methods correlates with the perfection of form.

The Buddhist path is presented within a general framework of what are called Ground, Path, and Fruition. First, we develop an understanding of the basic nature of reality in terms of two levels of reality, the conventional truth and the ultimate truth; this is the ground. Then, on the actual path, we gradually embody meditation and spiritual practice as a whole in terms of method and wisdom. The final fruition of one's spiritual path takes place in terms of the non-duality of perfected form and perfected wisdom.

The last two lines read:

And may I, recognizing all things as illusion,
Devoid of clinging, be released from bondage.

These lines actually point to the practice of cultivating insight into the nature of reality, but on the surface they seem to denote a way of relating to the world during the stages of post-meditation. In the Buddhist teachings on the ultimate nature of reality, two significant time periods are distinguished; one is the actual meditative session during which you remain in single-pointed meditation on emptiness, and the other is the period subsequent to the meditative session when you engage actively with the real world, as it were. So, here, these two lines directly concern the way of relating to the world in the aftermath of one's meditation on emptiness. This is why the text speaks of appreciating the illusion-like nature of reality, because this is the way one perceives things when one arises from single-pointed meditation on emptiness.

In my view, these lines make a very important point because sometimes people have the idea that what really matters is single-pointed meditation on emptiness within the meditative session. They pay much less attention to how this experience should be applied in post-meditation periods. However, I think the post-meditation period is very important. The whole point of meditating on the ultimate nature of reality is to ensure that you are not fooled by appearances, and that you appreciate the gap between how things appear to you and how they really are. Buddhism explains that appearances can often be deluding. With a deeper understanding of reality, you can go beyond appearances and relate to the world in a much more appropriate, effective, and realistic manner.

I often give the example of how we should relate to our neighbors. Imagine that you are living in a particular part of town where interaction with your neighbors is almost impossible, and yet it is actually better if you do interact with them rather than ignore them. To do so in the wisest way depends on how well you understand your neighbors' personality. If, for example, the man living next door is very resourceful, then being friendly and communicating with him will be to your benefit. At the same time, if you know that deep down he can also be quite tricky, that knowledge is invaluable if you are to maintain a cordial relationship and be vigilant so that he does not take advantage of you. Likewise, once you have a deeper understanding of the nature of reality, then in post-meditation, when you actually engage with the world, you will relate to people and things in a much more appropriate and realistic manner.

When the text refers to viewing all phenomena as illusions, it is suggesting that the illusion-like nature of things can only be perceived if you have freed yourself from attachment to phenomena as independent discrete entities. Once you have succeeded in freeing yourself from such attachment, the perception of the illusion-like nature of reality will automatically arise. Whenever things appear to you, although they appear to have an independent or objective existence, you will know as a result of your meditation that this is not really the case. You will be aware that things are not as substantial and solid as they seem. The term "illusion" therefore points to the disparity between how you perceive things and how they really are.

Generating the Mind for Enlightenment

For those who admire the spiritual ideals of the *Eight Verses on Transforming the Mind* it is helpful to recite the following verses for generating the mind for enlightenment. Practicing Buddhists should recite the verses and reflect upon the meaning of the words, while trying to enhance their altruism and compassion. Those of you who are practitioners of other religious traditions can draw from your own spiritual teachings, and try to commit yourselves to cultivating altruistic thoughts in pursuit of the altruistic ideal.

With a wish to free all beings	༄། འགྲོ་རྣམས་བསྒྲལ་འདོད་བསམ་པ་ཡིས།
I shall always go for refuge	སངས་རྒྱས་ཆོས་དང་དགེ་འདུན་ལ།
to the Buddha, Dharma and Sangha	བྱང་ཆུབ་སྙིང་པོར་མཆིས་ཀྱི་བར།
until I reach full enlightenment.	རྟག་པར་བདག་ནི་སྐྱབས་སུ་མཆི།
Enthused by wisdom and compassion,	ཤེས་རབ་སྙིང་བརྩེ་དང་བཅས་པས།
today in the Buddha's presence	བརྩོན་པས་སེམས་ཅན་དོན་དུ་བདག།
I generate the Mind for Full Awakening	སངས་རྒྱས་མདུན་དུ་གནས་བགྱིས་སྟེ།
for the benefit of all sentient beings.	རྫོགས་པའི་བྱང་ཆུབ་སེམས་བསྐྱེད་དོ།
As long as space endures,	ཇི་སྲིད་ནམ་མཁའ་གནས་པ་དང་།
as long as sentient beings remain,	འགྲོ་བ་ཇི་སྲིད་གནས་འགྱུར་པ།
until then, may I too remain	དེ་སྲིད་བདག་ནི་གནས་འགྱུར་ནས།
and dispel the miseries of the world.	འགྲོ་བའི་སྡུག་བསྔལ་སེལ་བར་ཤོག༎

In conclusion, those who, like myself, consider themselves to be followers of Buddha, should practice as much as we can. To followers of other religious traditions, I would like to say, "Please practice your own religion seriously and sincerely." And to nonbelievers, I request you to try to be warm-hearted. I ask this of you because these mental attitudes actually bring us happiness. As I have mentioned before, taking care of others actually benefits you.

THE EIGHT VERSES ON
TRANSFORMING THE MIND

Geshe Langri Thangpa

With a determination to achieve the highest aim
For the benefit of all sentient beings,
Which surpasses even the wish-fulfilling gem,
May I hold them dear at all times.

བདག་ནི་སེམས་ཅན་ཐམས་ཅད་ལ།
ཡིད་བཞིན་ནོར་བུ་ལས་ལྷག་པའི།
དོན་མཆོག་སྒྲུབ་པའི་བསམ་པ་ཡིས།
རྟག་ཏུ་གཅེས་པར་འཛིན་པར་ཤོག།

Whenever I interact with someone,
May I view myself as the lowest amongst all,
And, from the very depths of my heart,
Respectfully hold others as superior.

གང་དུ་སུ་དང་འགྲོགས་པའི་ཚེ།
བདག་ཉིད་ཀུན་ལས་དམན་པར་བལྟ་ཞིང་།
གཞན་ལ་བསམ་པ་ཐག་པ་ཡིས།
མཆོག་ཏུ་གཅེས་པར་འཛིན་པར་ཤོག།

In all my deeds may I probe into my mind,
And as soon as mental and emotional afflictions
    arise—

As they endanger myself and others—
May I strongly confront them and avert them.

སྤྱོད་ལམ་ཀུན་ཏུ་རང་རྒྱུད་ལ།
རྟོག་ཅིང་ཉོན་མོངས་སྐྱེས་མ་ཐག།
བདག་གཞན་མ་རུངས་བྱེད་པས་ན།
བཙན་ཐབས་གདོང་ནས་བཟློག་པར་ཤོག།

When I see beings of unpleasant character　　　རང་བཞིན་ངན་པའི་སེམས་ཅན་ནི།

Oppressed by strong negativity and suffering,　　སྡིག་སྡུག་དྲག་པོས་ནོན་མཐོང་ཚེ།

May I hold them dear—for they are rare to find—　རིན་ཆེན་གཏེར་དང་འཕྲད་པ་བཞིན།

As if I have discovered a jewel treasure!　　　རྙེད་པར་དཀའ་བའི་གཅེས་འཛིན་ཤོག།

When others, out of jealousy,　　　བདག་ལ་གཞན་གྱིས་ཕྲག་དོག་གིས།

Treat me wrongly with abuse, slander, and scorn,　གཤེ་སྐུར་ལ་སོགས་མི་རིགས་པའི།

May I take upon myself the defeat　　　གྱོང་ཁ་རང་གིས་ལེན་པ་དང་།

And offer to others the victory.　　　རྒྱལ་ཁ་གཞན་ལ་འབུལ་བར་ཤོག།

When someone whom I have helped,　　　གང་ལ་བདག་གིས་ཕན་བཏགས་པའི།

Or in whom I have placed great hopes,　　　རེ་བ་ཆེ་བ་གང་ཞིག་གིས།

Mistreats me in extremely hurtful ways,　　　ཤིན་ཏུ་མི་རིགས་གནོད་བྱེད་ནའང་།

May I regard him still as my precious teacher.　བཤེས་གཉེན་དམ་པར་བལྟ་བར་ཤོག།

In brief, may I offer benefit and joy　　　མདོར་ན་དངོས་དང་བརྒྱུད་པ་ཡིས།

To all my mothers, both directly and indirectly,　ཕན་བདེ་མ་རྣམས་ཀུན་ལ་འབུལ།

May I quietly take upon myself　　　མ་ཡི་གནོད་དང་སྡུག་བསྔལ་ཀུན།

All hurts and pains of my mothers.　　　གསང་བས་བདག་ལ་ལེན་པར་ཤོག།

May all this remain undefiled　　　དེ་དག་ཀུན་ཀྱང་ཆོས་བརྒྱད་ཀྱི།

By the stains of the eight mundane concerns;　རྟོག་པའི་དྲི་མས་མ་སྦགས་ཤིང་།

And may I, recognizing all things as illusion,　ཆོས་ཀུན་སྒྱུ་མར་ཤེས་པའི་བློས།

Devoid of clinging, be released from bondage.　ཞེན་མེད་འཆིང་བ་ལས་གྲོལ་ཤོག།

Appendix Two

ETHICS FOR THE NEW MILLENNIUM

Public Talk Given on May 10, 1999
at the Royal Albert Hall, London

INTRODUCTORY SPEECH BY LORD REES-MOGG, FORMER EDITOR OF *THE TIMES*

Your Holiness, Ladies and Gentlemen, it is a great and moving
honor to present the introductory speech on this occasion. Your
Holiness, you are seen in Britain as an inspired spiritual teacher
and very much as a friend, and you are surrounded by your friends
and admirers this evening. Your life has been one of the great lives
of spiritual teaching of our age, and like the life of other great spiritual teachers of this time, like that say of Mahatma Gandhi, it has
been not only a spiritual life, but a life necessarily involved in the
process of history and in the suffering of your people; and that is
something for which we have in Britain the greatest regard, the
greatest sympathy, and the greatest admiration.

Both in your own life and in the lives which your people have led, we recognize a combination of courage and compassion which is almost unique in the modern world. You have been a builder of bridges—a builder of bridges in international society, a builder of bridges between the great religions—and it is, I think, one of the marks of the quality of your teaching that you have combined a complete fidelity to your own religious tradition with a great understanding and love of the other religious traditions of the world.

This is now a very harsh period in the world, a period where again we seem to be threatened with wars and disturbances, and we are all conscious both of the plight of the people of Tibet and of the sufferings that are going on in Yugoslavia and particularly in Kosovo. In your latest book you put forward the ideas that you have already advanced for trying to create zones of peace in the world where there are the greatest fractures and dangers, and we welcome you this evening especially as a missionary for the idea that peace is the right way to solve the problems of the world. We recognize above everything else that your spiritual and ethical teaching has the certain marks of truth; the four marks are perhaps humility, humanity, endurance, and compassion. As a missionary of peace, as a spiritual teacher, we welcome you here this evening with our profound thanks.

His Holiness the Dalai Lama

Brothers and sisters, it is a great honor for me to have this opportunity to be with you today and to speak with you. I would like to take this opportunity to express my appreciation to the Tibet House Trust for organizing this event. I would also like to express my thanks to the members of the Tibetan community for their opening song, which made me remember my own homeland, Tibet. I would especially like to express my deep appreciation to Lord Rees-Mogg for his wonderful introductory speech. He praised me so much that I feel as if my feet are no longer on the ground. I also mean this literally—this chair is so high, my feet don't reach the floor! So may I take off my shoes and sit cross-legged? Ah, this is more comfortable.

I have spoken in this hall once before. I remember very clearly at that time one of my oldest and closest friends was here, the late Edward Carpenter, Dean of Westminster. I always had the deepest respect and admiration for him. Now he is no longer with us, but I still think of him, as I think of other old friends who are no longer here. There is a warm feeling which touches my heart and that always remains.

This shows us that time is moving on. Year by year, month by month, day by day, hour by hour, minute by minute, even second by second, it is always moving and never stands still. No force can stop that; it is beyond our control. All we can do is use time properly and constructively, or use it negatively and destructively. The choice is ours; the decision is in our own hands. So put your time to good use: I think that's very important. I believe that life is meant to bring us happiness. Negative actions always bring pain and sorrow, but constructive action brings us pleasure and joy.

Now tonight, some of you may have come here just out of curiosity, and that's fine. Then there are those of you who have come with some expectation: don't expect too much! I have nothing to offer you. Sometimes people come to see me with high expectations of some kind of miracle blessing or the like, and others see me as a healer. I often tell them that if I were a really good healer then I would not have the pimples I get these days; I cannot cure myself! So I don't think it is any good to harbor unrealistic expectations, and I want to make clear that we are all human beings, and the same as each other. I am no one special.

All human beings are basically the same, whether Easterners or Westerners, Southerners or Northerners, rich or poor, educated or uneducated, from this religion or that religion, believers or non-believers—as human beings, we are all fundamentally the same. Emotionally, mentally, physically, we are the same. Physically, maybe there are a few little differences in the shape of our noses, the colour of our hair and so on, but these are minor; basically, we are the same. And we have the same potential, the potential to transform our own mind and attitudes. For example, if today you are unhappy because you are afraid of something, or jealous, or angry, then all these reactions will make you more unhappy. On the other hand, today you might feel happy, and it might look as though you have nothing to worry about, but owing to some unforeseen conditions things could turn out badly.

We all have basically the same potential to undergo both positive and negative experiences. Furthermore, we also have the same potential to transform our attitudes.

It is very important to know that we can each transform ourselves into a better, happier person. I think it's important to recognize this.

Now, I have noticed that some people seem really excited about the new millennium. There is some kind of expectation that the new millennium itself will bring new and happier days. I feel that thinking is wrong. Unless there is some new millennium inside our hearts, then the external new millennium alone will not change much: we will still have the same days and nights, the same sun and moon, and so on. Last December I visited Paris briefly, and on the Eiffel Tower they had put a countdown of the number of days left this century. All this shows some kind of enthusiasm, a general looking forward to the new century. But then I thought, "What difference will the new century really make?" Actually, I think that life will carry on in the same way.

I would like to say that the most important thing is transforming our minds, so that we have a new way of thinking, and a new outlook. I think that we should make an effort to develop a new inner world. For centuries, and for generations, humanity has invested all its effort into developing society in terms of material facilities, on the basis of science and technology. I think today the world at large, and particularly the Western nations, have achieved very high living standards, yet a lot of problems remain, especially in the field of crime and violence. In England, America and elsewhere, some young people are even shooting others without much reason. And in the field of international relations, I often feel that nations which cherish freedom, democracy, and liberty very highly—even nations like America or Western European countries—in fact still rely very much on force.

I think these are old concepts. In the past, national interests were more or less independent of each other, and communities were largely self-sufficient even at the village level. In such circumstances, the concepts of war and military activity were quite relevant: if there is victory on our side, there will be defeat for the enemy on the other side. But today that situation has completely changed. Not only villages but nations and even continents are heavily interdependent, especially economically. Under these circumstances, to destroy your neighbor is actually to destroy yourself. So I think that we can now say that the old ways of thinking, and the policies that went with them, are outdated.

And then there is the question of lifestyle. Every year, we always expect there to be national growth, and if growth is stagnant then people feel there is something wrong. Sooner or later we will reach a point where we cannot go any further. Look at the gap between rich and poor. At the global level Northerners have a surplus, but Southerners are human beings just like Northerners, and both live together on the same planet, yet their basic needs are not met and they may even starve. Sometimes I think starvation is caused through their own mistakes; some of these nations put their wealth into military equipment rather than agriculture and so forth, and the result can be famine. And even within a very rich nation like America, there is a huge gap between billionaires and poor people. Some of my American friends recently told me that a few years ago the number of billionaires was around 15, I think, but now that figure is far higher. The number of billionaires has increased, but the poor still remain poor, and in some cases they are even poorer.

This huge gap between rich and poor at the global level, and within nations, is not only morally wrong but is also a source of practical problems. So we have to tackle these problems, and we have to raise the living standards of the South and of poorer people generally.

More than 15 years ago I visited a university in this country, and had a talk with an expert in environment and natural resources. He told me that if living standards in the South were raised to the standards which Northerners already enjoy, then with present population numbers, it was open to question whether the planet's natural resources would be sufficient. So, as I said, one way to tackle the problem is to raise living standards in poorer countries and within richer countries, but the consequence of that could be that sooner or later we will face the limits of our natural resources. This solution assumes that our lifestyle cannot be questioned, but I think, on the contrary, that it is worthwhile to look at it again.

Pollution is also a serious problem. To hold a few conferences on the issue here and there I think is very good, but real, effective implementation is needed. Once again, I think this issue is related to lifestyle. In America and also here in London, we see lots of cars on the road, but many of these cars carry just one person; it seems that almost every person has a car, and I think some families have two or three cars. Now just think of the Chinese population, over two billion, and of India's population of about 900 million. According to this model, there would be around three billion cars in those countries alone. That would be very difficult.

These are the problems. Sometimes I feel that it is not just me alone but millions of people who feel critical about the existing situation, but usually their voice is not clearly heard. So perhaps I am speaking on behalf of these millions of people who remain silent, or whose voice is weak. Unfortunately, we see the reality of our situation but there is a gap between our perception of it and our attitudes. I believe that reality has changed, but our thinking still remains the same, and that itself creates many problems.

Another point is that some of the problems that we are facing, in Kosovo or Northern Ireland or Indonesia, are not problems that have developed overnight; they have developed over decades, and in some cases over generations. I feel that in the initial stages, when there was more chance of changing the situation and cooling it down, people did not pay much attention. They ignored the problem, thinking maybe that it would not be so serious, or that the people directly involved ought to take care of it. Then later, when things became critical, it was too late. Once human emotions are out of control, they are very, very difficult to handle. In fact, according to the Buddhist understanding, when causes and conditions have evolved freely for a long period of time they reach a point when the process can no longer be reversed.

I feel that many of our problems develop in this way. During the initial stages there is more chance of reducing the problem, or eliminating it, or preventing it from becoming a crisis; but at that stage we neglect to address it. I also feel this about the Tibetan issue. In the twenties, thirties, and forties, I feel that the Tibetans themselves were very negligent about the future of their country. That's how it happens, and when it develops into a real crisis the situation explodes, and then it is too late.

Using force, of course, is a last resort. One aspect of violence is that it is unpredictable. Although your initial intention is to use limited force, once you have committed violence the consequences are unpredictable. Violence always creates unexpected implications and counter-violence, and it seems that this is exactly what is happening in Kosovo. So violence is, generally speaking, the wrong method, I think, particularly in this modern era.

Judging from these current events, there are real indications that something is wrong with our general attitude. If we develop the right attitude, I feel that we can reduce some of these problems, and other problems could even be eliminated. Many of our problems are essentially man-made, they are of our own creation, so if humanity were to use more appropriate methods with a far-sighted and more comprehensive view, then I think the situation could change quite quickly.

On the basis of the experience of this century, and of what we have learned from it, we should re-evaluate our attitudes, make more effort to improve things, and then perhaps the next century will be a happier, more peaceful, and more friendly one. This is my firm belief. At least compared to the early part of this century, I think today, generally speaking, there have been positive changes in our outlook; there are signs that we are developing a wider perspective. We could say that humanity is becoming more mature. So if we continue to make tireless efforts in this direction, mainly through education, I think the next millennium could be more peaceful. However, for this to be the case we must prepare well. If we fully prepare ourselves, then I think it is worthwhile to be excited about the new millennium, but unless some change occurs within ourselves, any expectation that the new year itself will bring a big change is unrealistic.

The future of humanity depends on the present generation, so each one of us has the responsibility of thinking about the future. In that context, I always try to share the following point with my audience: that the future of humanity is very largely dependent on our own thinking and behavior.

Earlier, I mentioned the importance of education. Modern education is very good, but it seems to be based on a universal acceptance of the importance of developing the brain, that is, on intellectual education. Insufficient attention is given to the development of the person as a whole, in the sense of becoming a good person or developing a warm heart. I think that a separate educational institution was established in Europe about a thousand years ago, and at that time it was the Church and the family that took care of moral education and the nurturing of human warmth. In that way, education was quite balanced. But as time went on, the influence of the Church decreased, and family life sometimes became unstable or problematic, so that in recent times this important aspect of children's upbringing has been neglected. It seems as if there is no particular institution that has special responsibility for taking care of the heart.

I think it's quite clear that education or knowledge is like an instrument, and whether that instrument is put to use in a constructive or destructive way depends on each person's motivation. An education system that cultivates smart brains alone can sometimes create more problems, and from the individual's point of view, having too many clever thoughts and too much imagination can even lead to a nervous breakdown.

If a child with a good intellectual education happens to have parents with a warm heart, and a sense of responsibility for both caring and discipline, then these can go together well and be very constructive. It is my hope that in future, the educational system will pay more attention to the development of human warmth and love. I think that's necessary. Right from kindergarten up to university, I think it is important to address moral questions related to the whole life of the individual, including his or her role in society and in the family. Without that, you can't be a happy person, you can't have a happy family, and so you can't have a happy society. Parents, too, have a special responsibility in this area. And I hope that in future there will be fewer divorces, particularly between couples who have children. For children especially I think it is very important for the parents to have a long-lasting happy marriage; that way, through their own practice and example, they will introduce their children to the benefits of love, kindness, and a warm heart.

I would like to add that I think it's very useful to introduce children to the idea that whenever they are faced with a conflict situation, the best and most practical way of resolving it is through dialogue, not violence. Violence means one side has victory and the other side defeat, but that's not realistic in today's world, as I mentioned earlier. If interests were clear-cut, and my interest were independent of yours, then defeat and victory would work; but today, everyone's interests are so intertwined that this is impossible. Therefore the only solution is a 50–50 compromise, if possible, or perhaps 60–40! Since there is no possibility of one side having a clear-cut victory, dialogue is essential. In order to solve a problem you have to appreciate what is at stake for your opponents, take care of their interests as well as you can, and in that light try to find a solution. I think it is good to introduce the idea of dialogue into schools from an early age, and train students to debate different views. In this way they will practice debating, and the concept of dialogue will gradually be instilled in them. Dialogue is the appropriate method, the effective method, the realistic method.

There will always be conflicts and disagreements in human society. Even within ourselves, we may find that we are fully convinced of one idea in the morning, but by the afternoon we have another idea, and there can be an inner conflict between the two.

Sometimes this can be extremely difficult; intense inner conflict can sometimes lead to suicide. So whenever you have two conflicting ideas, the wise way is to think through both sides of the argument and then find a synthesis which overcomes contradictions and conflicts. I think there are contradictory forces in everyone, but if we can bring them together and find a balance, then we have made progress. Furthermore, if we can assess contradictory views wisely and overcome the contradiction, then new ideas will come, so in this sense contradiction itself is not bad. In fact, it can be the basis for further development. It is only if it gets out of control and is expressed violently that it becomes destructive.

Once the student has developed a good habit, then as soon as there is conflict he or she will immediately respond by way of dialogue rather than violence or fighting. I tell some audiences that through such training, it's possible that when a student returns from school and finds his parents quarrelling, he might manage to persuade them that this is wrong. I think that through such training, one day we will all be clear that human beings are social animals, and our individual interests rest on society; therefore each individual should be a warm-hearted, sensible person, and a good citizen. That will bring peace of mind at the individual level, at family level, and at the level of the community. Whenever differences arise, we will discuss them together and share our anxieties with each other in a peaceful and friendly way.

The development of that kind of attitude is related to basic human values, that is, a sense of caring, a sense of responsibility, and a sense of forgiveness. We could call them basic spiritual values. Whether we believe in a religion or not is a matter of individual choice, but regardless of whether or not we have a religious faith, so long as we are human beings, and so long as we are part of human society, without these good human qualities we cannot be happy. The very purpose of life is to find happiness, so there is no point in neglecting those very things which are directly related to making us happy.

We can call these basic human values "secular ethics," since they do not depend on religious faith. "Secular" here does not mean we necessarily reject religion, but rather that religious faith is an individual matter.

I think we really need to make more of an effort to promote these basic human values. There is good reason to develop these qualities, because basically I believe that human nature is gentle. There are different opinions on this, of course; some say human nature is aggressive. But judging from our life as a whole, from the beginning of our life up to death, I think aggression is only occasional. On the other hand, I think that the whole of our life is very much involved with love and affection.

For example, our physical constitution is such that even the cells of our body work better if we have peace of mind, whereas an agitated mind usually brings some physical imbalance. If peace of mind is important for good health, that means the body itself is structured in a way that accords with mental peace. Therefore we can say that human nature is more inclined to gentleness and affection. Even our body structure seems designed not for fighting but for embracing. Look at our hands: if they were meant for hitting, I think they would be hard like a hoof. More importantly, according to medical science, the weeks immediately after birth are very crucial for our development, because the brain is growing very rapidly, and during that period physical contact—with one's mother or someone else—is one of the most important factors for the healthy development of the brain. This shows that even physically we thrive on others' affection. All these responses show that we need human affection.

On the mental level, too, we find that the more compassionate we are, the more we have peace of mind. The moment we think about others our mind becomes broader and more open, and then our personal problems appear insignificant. On the other hand, if you think just about "me, me, me," your whole mental focus becomes very narrow and closed, and even tiny problems seem huge. When you think about others' welfare and share their suffering, at that moment you may feel unhappy or disturbed, but you take this on voluntarily. Deep inside, you have courage, self-confidence, and inner strength when you care for the suffering of others. In contrast, when you suffer from problems that arise involuntarily, the experience of suffering overwhelms you. So there is a big difference between the two experiences.

According to my own little experience, the more I meditate on compassion and think about the infinite number of sentient beings who are suffering, the more I have an immense feeling of inner strength. Then the problems I may have, here and there, don't matter so much. The more we have inner strength and self-confidence, the more this reduces fear and doubt, and this automatically makes us more open. Then we can communicate with our human brothers and sisters everywhere much more easily, because when you are open, others will respond accordingly. On the other hand, when we have fear, hatred or doubt, the door to our heart is closed; then we will relate to everyone with suspicion. I think the worst thing is to experience suspicion and doubt; you get the impression that other people also have similar suspicions or doubts about you, and as a result you become more and more distant. This ends in loneliness and frustration.

This is why I think that compassion and caring for others are really wonderful things. The problem is that usually people think that the message of compassion, love, and forgiveness is a religious one, so those who have no special interest in religion tend to neglect these values. I think that's wrong. We must all pay more attention to these values. That is one way we can prepare for the next millennium.

My second main point is the critical importance of inter-religious harmony and understanding. Religious faith is unique to human beings, for in the animal kingdom there is no such thing as a religious belief. Faith can be useful if you use it properly, but if you do not use it properly it can bring disaster. The reason for this is that religious faith involves human emotions, and sometimes our emotions can go wrong; then there is no room for reason and we become fanatics or fundamentalists. This is why we need to put more effort into ensuring that all the major world religions harness the human potential for the betterment of humanity—to serve humanity, and to save the planet—while, in the meantime, we try to reduce conflict waged in the name of religion.

For a few years now I have been practicing various methods to achieve this, and some of my spiritual brothers and sisters from other faiths are also now joining me in this.

The first method is to arrange meetings between scholars of the different traditions, to discuss the differences and similarities primarily at the academic level.

The second method is to arrange meetings of serious practitioners of the various religions, where they can exchange their inner experiences. This is very, very powerful, and extremely helpful in understanding the value of traditions other than one's own. In my own case, I have met with the late Thomas Merton and other serious practitioners, and meeting with these people really opened my eyes to the value of other traditions. This method is very helpful for developing mutual understanding and mutual respect.

The third method is multi-faith pilgrimage. A group of people from different religious traditions visit the holy places of the various traditions together. If possible, they pray together, and if not they just sit in silent meditation. Pilgrimages like this are an immensely valuable and deep experience. On one occasion I visited Lourdes, in southern

France, not as a tourist but as a pilgrim. I drank the holy water and stood in front of Mary's statue, and I thought to myself that here, in this place, millions of people who are seeking blessing or tranquillity find satisfaction on this spot. As I looked at the statue of Mary, a deep feeling of admiration and appreciation for Christianity rose within me, simply because it provides so much benefit to millions of people. Christianity may have a different philosophy, but that's another question. The practical value of the help and benefit it offers is quite clear.

So I have found it very useful to experience a deeper feeling about other religions through the atmosphere of these sacred places. A number of Christians have already responded to this proposal, and last year some of my Christian brothers and sisters came and spent a few days in Bodh Gaya. We had a dialogue between Buddhists and Christians, and each morning under the Bodhi Tree we all sat together and meditated. I think that was historic. Since Buddha's coming more than 2,500 years ago, and since Jesus Christ's coming almost 2,000 years ago, I think that is the first time such a meeting has taken place.

The fourth method is to organize gatherings like the one held in Assisi, Italy, in the mid-eighties. Religious leaders from several faiths come together, recite prayers from the same platform, and exchange a few words on a particular theme (in Assisi, the theme was the environment). This sort of event can be very significant for the millions of followers of each religion, when they see their own leaders taking part in such a friendly exchange and delivering the same message of peace as other faiths. So these are the four methods I suggest we follow in order to foster religious harmony.

There is another point I would like to share with you tonight. We have talked about promoting a sense of caring for others, of sharing others' problems, and trying to reduce hatred. We should not leave any room for hatred, either individually, within the family, in society, or even in humanity as a whole, because hatred is the real destroyer of our peace and happiness. What we need is something like an inner disarmament. With inner disarmament, and an awareness of the effects of war, then the concept of military activity and destruction becomes outdated.

On this basis, we have to think seriously about how to reduce weapons. First we should tackle nuclear weapons, and fortunately there are already programs for dismantling nuclear warheads, and that is a wonderful start. Such programs should not only limit the number of warheads, but I think it is important that they also seek the total destruction of nuclear weapons, so still more effort is needed. Then, step by step, I think the world should eventually be free of the military establishment, and we should have a demilitarized world. I think that should be our long-term target. I am not saying that we should disarm overnight; in some cases I think it may take generations, but I think it is worthwhile to have that kind of blueprint in mind.

Of course, there will always be a few mischievous human beings around, so in order to counter them there needs to be some kind of international force. We already have something of this kind in the international peacekeeping force under the United Nations. First, we should establish a limited military force on a regional basis, consisting of a small number of good quality, effective mobile forces, and this should be controlled by all member states. If disputes arise, this force can act as a countermeasure. However, no nation would have an independent military force of its own. One example of this is Costa Rica, which for more than 50 years has enjoyed a demilitarized state.

In this way, I think that inner disarmament and external disarmament go together.

I think the first advantage it will bring is that it will save a lot of money. Each bomb and each cruise missile is enormously expensive, so if a conflict lasts weeks or months, very large sums are involved. Instead of wasting our money and using it for destructive purposes, I think we should use it more constructively. Just imagine if this money went to build hospitals or schools in poorer countries, how beneficial that could be.

Not only could we save a lot of money, we could also prevent a certain degree of pollution. Sometimes I say jokingly that those factories which produce tanks could easily make bulldozers instead; and then the scientists who work in the military field, and who up to now have focused their knowledge and their marvellous brains on developing various means of destruction, could shift to a more constructive field. When they do this, it would be worthwhile giving them double pay!

We have to think along these lines if we are concerned about the benefit and happiness of humanity in the future. So I think there should be less excitement about the new millennium and more inward thinking, more attention paid to preparing ourselves for it. At my age, I think I belong to this century, and eventually I will be ready to say goodbye, so it is the younger generation who will really shape the next century. So all you younger people should reflect very carefully, without emotion and without attachment, from a wide perspective and with a long-sighted view. This is very, very important.

This is the end of my talk. If you feel some points are worth investigating further, then please do so. On the other hand, if you feel the points I have made are not so relevant, or just nonsense, then forget about them and just leave them behind in this hall! Thank you very much.

QUESTIONS

Question: Your Holiness, I struggle with my thoughts about the war in Kosovo. On the one hand I don't want to countenance any killing, but I don't think the West should ignore the situation either. I am mindful of this same situation in Tibet, Burma, Rwanda, and so on. Are we not responsible for our Government's actions? How do we act now to ease the suffering of Serbs and Kosovar Albanians?

HHDL: Over recent weeks many people have put this question to me, particularly people from that area who are eagerly seeking my advice. But I am no expert. My knowledge is only based on newspaper reports, and so on. The fact that Western organizations like NATO are showing concern about human rights violations in Kosovo and the suffering of the Kosovo people is of course very good; so is their attempt to stop ethnic cleansing, which is such a terrible policy. Some of the older generation still have a clear memory of the horrible genocide practiced by the Nazis during the Second World War. So the response of these nations is I think very encouraging and very good, but the method they are using is force. Basically, I am always against the use of force, for the reasons I have outlined.

What is the alternative? What alternative is there to stop these human miseries under the present circumstances? I don't know. It's very difficult. In my opinion, as I mentioned earlier, it is now too late; I think we really missed our opportunity earlier on. But on the basis of our experience of Kosovo, we should now pay more attention to other regions of the globe where there is the possibility of crisis in the future, and we should take preventive measures.

Question: Your Holiness, there is more and more pressure on
young people to compete academically in the West
because of the shortage of jobs and the lack of
spiritual balance. How can this change? Don't you
think we have gone too far and that it is difficult to
reverse the process?

HHDL: I don't think it's too late, as I said earlier. If, as a
society, we make attempts to change our basic ways
of thinking and dealing with issues, and if society as a
whole changes, there is still potential. No matter how
difficult it is, we should not lose hope and
confidence. It is very, very important to keep
optimistic. If, from the outset, you feel you can't do
anything because there are difficulties, then that
self-defeatist, pessimistic attitude becomes the real
source of failure. It doesn't matter whether or not
you achieve your goal within a short period, or even
within this present lifetime: if something is really
worthwhile, you should attempt it. Then, at least, you
will have no regrets. If we withdraw because things
are difficult, eventually we always regret it.

Question: Do you support the idea of a universal faith, a
universal religion?

HHDL: What do you mean by that? That all religions
should be unified? Sometimes I call compassion the
universal religion. But if you mean it in the sense that

we should create a universal religion with some ideas from one religion and some ideas from another, I think that is foolish. It is much better to keep the different religious traditions distinct so that each religion remains unique. Then the variety of philosophies and the variety of traditions will satisfy a variety of people. I think the very reason why so many different world religions arose in the first place is because people are different, and have different mental dispositions. A single religion would never satisfy everyone, so it is much better to have a number of traditions.

At the same time, as I mentioned, there are some fundamental differences between religions. Recently in Argentina, I took part in a university dialogue on religion and science with a bishop, a scientist and a medical scientist. When my turn came, I just casually mentioned that in Buddhism there is no concept of a "Creator" so the law of causality is said to be beginningless. Afterwards, the bishop expressed surprise, because he had thought that even Buddhism accepted God as a Creator. "Oh," he said, "then there's no basis for dialogue between Christianity and Buddhism." He said it in a very jovial way.

So I told him that yes, there are fundamental differences, yet there are common practices, and a common message like the message of compassion,

love, forgiveness, and contentment. Both religions
also have the same purpose. To some people the
concept of the Creator is very powerful, as this
Creator is full of compassion and mercy, and this
very life we have was created by Him. This idea
brings a feeling of intimacy with God, so we feel that
in order to fulfill God's wish, we ourselves should be
compassionate. Any genuine Christian should show
genuine love and compassion towards his fellow
human beings. That is the real meaning of the love of
God. If someone doesn't bother to practice love and
compassion towards his fellows, but at the same time
says, "God is great," I think that is hypocritical. In
order to be a good Christian, you should practice
compassion, love and forgiveness and, as the Bible
says, if someone hits you, you should turn the other
cheek. This is what we call the practice of tolerance in
Buddhism. So there are many similarities between
Christianity and Buddhism.

When we look at the purpose of these different
traditions, then we can see it is the same, and based
on the same potential. The Buddhist and Jain idea
that there is no Creator, and that everything depends
on one's own responsibility, is simply a more effective
approach for certain people. So we could say that
each religion has a unique way of producing good
human beings.

Question: Your Holiness, sometimes it seems that the choices
we make are predetermined by causes and
conditions. How far are we really free to choose?

HHDL: When we talk about the law of cause and effect, we
are talking about a universal principle that applies to
all things and events. Everything comes into being as
a result of causes and conditions. In the particular
context of the experience of living beings, we are
talking of a situation where the actions of an
individual are part of the causal process. The fact
that individuals are active agents participating in the
causal process implies that they are conscious beings
with some choice about the actions that they
perform. There is also another level of choice:
although one may have committed a particular
action which has set a certain course of events in
motion, that causal action alone is not enough for
fruition to take place. Circumstances and other
auxiliary conditions are needed to activate the
cause and bring it to complete fruition. In this
respect, we have some freedom in controlling
or at least influencing these circumstances and
conditions.

Question: Your Holiness, capital punishment has always been
an issue of popular debate. What are your feelings on
this subject?

HHDL: I'm against the death penalty. I think it is bad, and it makes me very sad. Whenever I see photographs of convicted prisoners who are condemned to death row, I feel very disturbed and uncomfortable.

You see, basically I think that everybody has afflictive emotions; the potential for hatred or forceful anger is there within all of us. Because of the circumstances, something happened for these poor people and they acted on those emotions, but I think they have the potential for good in them as well. For this reason, it is best not to reject criminals mentally, but to bring them back into society and give them a chance to improve themselves and change. I have heard that in Tihar Jail, in India, the authorities introduced a meditation course for the prisoners which had a tremendous effect; many people really changed. In America, too, volunteers are helping prisoners by giving them some spiritual training. Amnesty International is campaigning for a total ban on capital punishment, and I have signed that.

Question: Where does anger come from?
HHDL: [Laughs] I think each philosophy has a different explanation. From the Buddhist viewpoint, anger basically comes from ignorance. More immediately, I think anger comes from attachment; the more attachment we have, the more likely we are to get angry.

Anger, just like other negative emotions, is part of our minds, but on the other hand compassion, loving-kindness and altruism are also part of our minds. So what is important is to analyze our thoughts. What thoughts are useful? What thoughts are harmful? After we have examined ourselves in this way, we discover that some thoughts contradict each other: for example, anger and hatred contradict loving-kindness. Then we ask ourselves what the benefit of hatred is, and what is the benefit of loving-kindness. If you feel loving-kindness is useful, then you can try to increase it as a counter-measure against hatred and anger. If the number of these thoughts increases, then the number of their opposing thoughts will be reduced. That's the way to train your mind.

Without such a training, everyone has negative thoughts and has positive thoughts, and both are equally strong. Certain conditions provoke negative emotions while others provoke positive ones. However, by making a conscious effort we can change that pattern, and this is what we mean by transforming the mind. It is a way to improve ourselves. I think that irrespective of whether you are a believer or a non-believer, the more you nurture a feeling of loving-kindness, the happier and calmer you will be. Your basic outlook will remain calm, and even if you hear a disturbing piece of news, it will not disturb you too much. So this is a very useful approach. On the other hand, if you are predominantly unhappy on account of hatred or certain negative thoughts you harbor, then even when good news comes your way it might disturb you even more.

Since we are all looking for a happy life, I think it is really worth thinking about these questions and examining our thoughts. We should then try to put our good thoughts to the best use possible, and try to minimize our negative ones. In this way we will train our minds. I think it would be useful for everyone to carry out such an experiment. No matter whether we are rich or poor, we all have the same type of brain, and we all have the same laboratory to work with in our head and heart. And this experiment doesn't cost anything; everything is here, within ourselves. Even poor people, even beggars can do this. In fact, in the past, some of the great masters in Tibet lived as beggars, but their minds and hearts were full of richness.

RECOMMENDED READING

The Dalai Lama, *Kindness, Clarity and Insight* (translated and edited by Jeffrey Hopkins), Snow Lion, New York, 1984.

The Dalai Lama, *A Flash of Lightning in the Dark of Night: A guide to the Bodhisattva's Way of Life* (translated by the Padmakara Translation Group), Shambhala, USA, 1994.

The Dalai Lama, *The Power of Compassion* (translated and edited by Geshe Thupten Jinpa), Thorsons, London, 1995.

The Dalai Lama, *Four Noble Truths* (translated by Geshe Thupten Jinpa; edited by Dominique Side), Thorsons, London, 1998

The Dalai Lama, *Heart of Buddha's Path* (translated by Geshe Thupten Jinpa), Thorsons, London, 1999

The Dalai Lama, *Ancient Wisdom, Modern World – Ethics for the New Millennium*, Little, Brown and Co., London, 1999

Jay Garfield, *The Fundamental Wisdom of the Middle Way*
(translation of Nagarjuna's *Mulamadhyamakakarika*),
Oxford University Press, Oxford, 1995.

The Library of Tibet, *Way to Freedom*, Thorsons, London, 1995

The Library of Tibet, *Awakening Mind, Lightening Heart*,
Thorsons, London, 1997

Nagarjuna and the 7th Dalai Lama, *The Precious Garland and the
Song of the Four Mindfulnesses*, (translated by Jeffrey Hopkins),
Wisdom of Tibet Series 2, George Allen & Unwin, London,
1975.

Shantideva: translations of his *Bodhicaryavatara* include:
The Way of the Bodhisattva (translated by the Padmakara
Translation Group), Shambhala, USA, 1997; and *The
Bodhicharyavatara* (translated by Kate Crosby and Andrew
Skilton) Oxford University Press, Oxford, 1996.

༄༅། །བཀའ་གདམས་པའི་དགེ་བ་ཤེས་སྐྱང་རེ་ཐར་པ་རྟེ་རྗེ་མེད་གོས་
མཛད་པའི་བློ་སྦྱོང་ཚིགས་བཅད་མ་བཞུགས་སོ།།

༡   བདག་ནི་སེམས་ཅན་ཐམས་ཅད་ལ།
    ཡིད་བཞིན་ནོར་བུ་ལས་ལྷག་པའི།
    དོན་མཆོག་སྒྲུབ་པའི་བསམ་པ་ཡིས།
    རྟག་ཏུ་གཅེས་པར་འཛིན་པར་ཤོག།

༢   གང་དུ་སུ་དང་གྲོགས་པའི་ཚེ།
    བདག་ཉིད་ཀུན་ལས་དམན་བལྟ་ཞིང་།
    གཞན་ལ་བསམ་པ་ཐག་པ་ཡིས།
    མཆོག་ཏུ་གཅེས་པར་འཛིན་པར་ཤོག།

༣   སྤྱོད་ལམ་ཀུན་ཏུ་རང་རྒྱུད་ལ།
    རྟོག་ཅིང་ཉོན་མོངས་སྐྱེས་མ་ཐག།
    བདག་གཞན་མ་རུངས་བྱེད་པས་ན།
    བཙན་ཐབས་གདོང་ནས་བཟློག་པར་ཤོག།

༤   རང་བཞིན་ངན་པའི་སེམས་ཅན་ནི།
    སྡིག་སྒྲུབ་དྲག་པོས་ནོན་མཛོད་ཚེ།
    རིན་ཆེན་གཏེར་དང་འཕྲད་པ་བཞིན།
    རྙེད་པར་དཀའ་བའི་གཅེས་འཛིན་ཤོག།

༥   བདག་ལ་གཞན་གྱིས་ཕྲག་དོག་གིས།
    གཤེ་སྐུར་ལ་སོགས་མི་རིགས་པའི།
    གྱོང་ཁ་རང་གིས་ལེན་པ་དང་།
    རྒྱལ་ཁ་གཞན་ལ་འབུལ་བར་ཤོག།

༦   གང་ལ་བདག་གིས་ཕན་བཏགས་པའི།
    རེ་བ་ཆེ་བ་གང་ཞིག་གིས།
    ཤིན་ཏུ་མི་རིགས་གནོད་བྱེད་ནའང་།
    བཤེས་གཉེན་དམ་པར་བལྟ་བར་ཤོག།

༧   མདོར་ན་དངོས་དང་བརྒྱུད་པ་ཡིས།
    ཕན་བདེ་མ་རྣམས་ཀུན་ལ་འབུལ།
    མ་ཡི་གནོད་དང་སྡུག་བསྔལ་ཀུན།
    གསང་བས་བདག་ལ་ལེན་པར་ཤོག།

༨   དེ་དག་ཀུན་ཀྱང་ཚོས་བརྒྱད་ཀྱི།
    རྟོག་པའི་དྲི་མས་མ་སྦགས་ཤིང་།
    ཚོས་ཀུན་སྒྱུ་མར་ཤེས་པའི་བློས།
    ཞེན་མེད་འཆིང་བ་ལས་གྲོལ་ཤོག།